TARUN TAHILIANI

JOURNEY TO INDIA MODERN

TARUN TAHILIANI

JOURNEY TO INDIA MODERN

FOREWORD: Fern Mallis

—

ESSAYS: Alia Allana

DESIGN: Pallavi Nopany

—

DESIGN CONSULTANT: Sneha Pamneja

CONTRIBUTION: Nonita Kalra & Sujata Assomull

Lustre Press
Roli Books

Shades of metallic sequins, pearl and *resham* lehenga adorned with Swarovski pavé bralette. An Italian tulle and crystal wraparound embellished with pearls and feathers.
COUTURE 2022

ACKNOWLEDGMENTS

"THIS ISN'T MY JOURNEY ALONE"

Even at the heights of delicious joy, Oscar speeches often sound bizarre—a frantic rambling of emotional thanks! So, imagine having to acknowledge and thank people who, in one way or another, helped me on this journey, which lasted much longer than any film!

I wish to thank my aunts who I painted with, art teachers like Mrs. Dutta we workshopped with, my mother Jaswanti who sent me to every art class possible, and museums and artists who expanded my vision. I thank my sister Tina who I threw the Ensemble keys to when I went to study; and Sal, my wife who pushed me ahead and often was the lone voice who would tell me what things really were. This started when I saw her in a Pierre Cardin show; at that time, I sold oil-field equipment for a living.

My first clothes were made with Kundalini, Naseem Khan and Bapa Dhrangadhra. In addition to them, I thank the masterjis, embroiderers, people who inspired us to reach for the stars, muses, and friends like Minal Modi and Simi Garewal who sat there night after night sharing their myriad visions, ideas, and the mentoring by friends like Rohit Khosla who shared every last experience they had gleaned, and Martand Singh (Mapu) with all his wealth of textile knowledge, Anil Chopra, Lakmè, Sumeet, Fern, Ritu, and, of course, my fantastic and passionate design teams that made it happen. Apart from all the people who spoke wonderful words of encouragement or advice, there were some who also in their negativity were instrumental in teaching me great lessons. I thank them too. A great professor at school congratulated me for winning the "Best Artist Prize", but asked where I thought I would get with drawing high fashion models. I was stumped! I had no idea. I drew because I loved it, and the ideas flowed out of me. And here I am—40 years on—still drawing them, all sorts of things, on any scrap of paper. I loved it then and still do.

I suppose that was enough, the rest is a bonus! Stars come and go, collections are loved or not, but the consciousness of what we carry forward, integrating culture, craft, cosmic energy, and history into something, is what this book tries to capture! Like everything, it was a journey.

Anand, my son, reignited it, with Anthony Thottingill firing off the shoulder.

As I reflect on the remarkable individuals who have played a significant role in our journey, names like Kiran and

"My parents at their wedding in February 1960."

"Rajiv Gandhi (*left*) at our wedding reception in December 1985. We began Ensemble a year later, in 1986."

"My father, Admiral R.H. Tahiliani, was Chief of Naval Staff. As a result, I had a diverse upbringing of military rigour, boarding school, and the arts, thanks to my mother."

Pushpa Renu come to mind. However, our current team includes exceptional talents such as Dolly Roy, Sonu Sehgal, Shadman Haider, and our esteemed design, embroidery, and department heads. This factory may not have existed today were it not for them and Basant Khatri, and Admiral Talwar.

In my long innings, some irreplaceable spokes that have held up the wheel have been: Ratna Vyas, Manish Vasvani, Gautam Rakha, Dilnaz Kharbay, Rakesh Aggarwal, Mansha Sahni, Ghazala, Yogesh, Aseem Kapoor, Nishant Vashisht, Anupama Bose, and many more. A design studio is an ecosystem. The retail is run by Manoj Sharma, Ekta Kaushik and the ateliers by Ajju, Umerjit, Arshad, Rehman, Azeem Bhai, Manoranjan and more... the list is endless. So many more both in the past and today. I also wish to thank Archana, the lovely Simar, and Prabh who brought the clothes to life.

I owe my gratitude to Rohit Chawla for opening this door, Pallavi Nopany for working, reworking, and redoing the layouts in pursuit of the intangible, and, of course, Alia Allana who talked to every single person along the way to document what made it, what it all meant, and where it is going!

I am sure there are hundreds more who need to be mentioned. To those whom I have missed, please forgive my omission! While it is not possible to mention each person here, it does not diminish their contributions.

This conversation started with Sal, my partner, wife, and friend at a shoot in February 1987. Many leaps of faith were taken, tried, lost, and more as it evolved and now, we move on to the next phase. Finally, I give thanks to my parents who always encouraged me and let me love art for the sake of it. I am grateful for all that we were and more.

Finally, I would like to express my deepest gratitude to my publisher, Priya Kapoor, and the exceptional team at Roli Books. Throughout the arduous journey of this book, under the peculiar and protracted circumstances, I often found myself devoid of motivation. However, Priya tirelessly propelled me forward with her unwavering determination, providing objective yet constructive criticism with a touch of sweetness. I am also grateful to Bipin Shah, who embarked on this journey with me, and Mita Kapoor, who guided us along the way.

The press, along with influencers like Isabella Blow, and countless friends from distant lands, have also contributed to our story. The list of these remarkable individuals has grown so long that it becomes a challenge to mention them all. Nevertheless, their invaluable contributions will always be cherished and remembered.

Special thanks to Tarun Vishwa and Gautam Kalra for the 25th anniversary shoot.

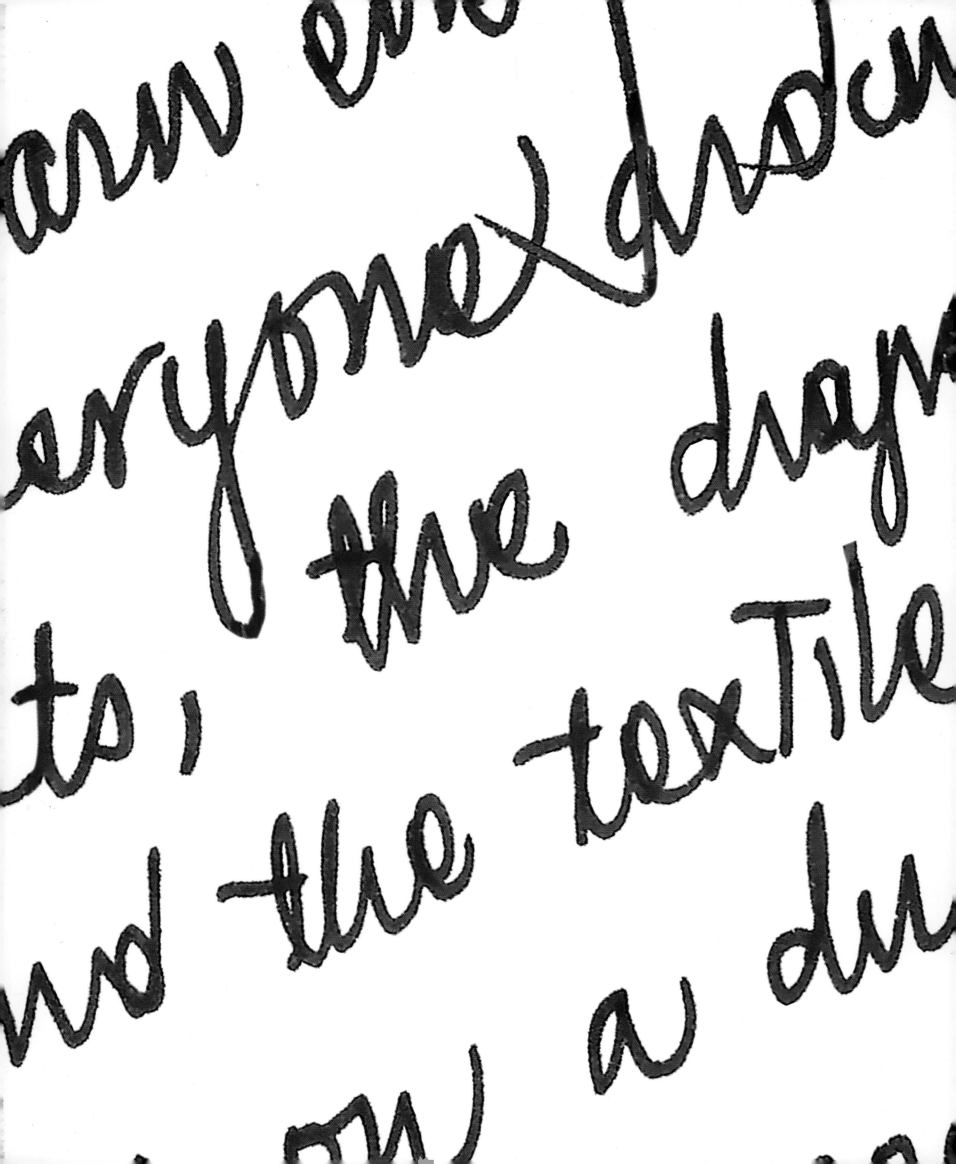

It takes many pairs
of hands to achieve
perfection in a last
fitting. Here, we are
doing a fitting for
actress Kriti Sanon."

"I want to look like I am wrapped in a turban."

MINAL MODI

"Minal Modi was my most serious studio muse. She loved clothes. She would come to the studio and try outfits before significant collections were released to give us feedback. She taught us techniques such as corsetry and certain kinds of embroidery—it was a perfect jugalbandi. Her statement, 'I want to look like I am wrapped in a turban', began my journey with drape."

FOREWORD

"TARUN TAHILIANI WAS MY INTRODUCTION TO INDIAN FASHION..."

FERN MALLIS

Former Executive Director,
Council of Fashion Designers of America

Tarun Tahiliani was my introduction to Indian fashion and the realm of Indian fashion designers. Tahiliani has left an indelible mark on my life, my career, and my wardrobe.

In July 2001, I joined IMG, the global marketing, management, and events powerhouse as Senior Vice President of Fashion after leaving my position as Executive Director at the Council of Fashion Designers of America (CFDA). Earlier the same year, IMG had acquired 7th on Sixth (also known as New York Fashion Week), which I, along with Stan Herman, had been instrumental in organizing and creating in 1993. This edition of 7th on Sixth completely changed the fashion landscape in the US and ultimately around the world. This was the first time American designers' collections were organized, modernized, and centralized to be staged in tents in New York's Bryant Park. It was also the first time fashion shows were sponsored by corporate partners.

Five weeks after assuming this new position, and suffering from a severe attack of diverticulitis, IMG had me booked on an Air India flight to Bombay to attend their first Fashion Week, which was presented by Lakmè, the leading cosmetic company in the country. I was nervous about my health and the idea of travelling to this very far away, exotic country. My doctor told me I could eat only clear foods, soups, broths—anything I could see through. I imagined it would not be an easy feat, especially in India. She also added, "If you get sick, I'm happy that you'll be in India and not England... They have better doctors there."

So, I packed up my most fashionable New York summer clothes to fly to India for what became the first of more than 60 trips to this very special country. My flight arrived in Bombay (the old airport) and, immediately, I breathed in the fragrance of India. Tired and jet-lagged, I made my

way to the Taj Mahal Palace Hotel. My eyes were wide open for the entire hour-and-a-half trip, taking it all in—the crowded roads, markets, people walking everywhere, the colourful saris, the constantly honking horns, the slums, the streets of broken stones and piles of trash, the dogs, the cats, the occasional cow, and the many children. Arriving at the Taj, majestically situated on the Arabian Sea and across the road from the Gateway of India, I felt like Cinderella at the ball. The lobby at that hour was comparable to New York's Grand Central Station, bustling, busy, music was playing, lounges were full, glasses were clinking, people were laughing and partying.... After all, it was headquarters for the Fashion Week shows. I instantly fell in love with this landmark, historic hotel, and went on to eventually stay there more nights than I can ever count over a period of almost 15 years.

The next morning there was a breakfast organized to introduce me to the designers and select fashion press in India, many of whom are my dearest friends to this day. Then, I met Tarun Tahiliani. He was larger than life, erudite, articulate, fast-talking, knowledgeable and oh-so charming. He was a clear leader, which explained why others deferred to him literally as "the leader". I knew we would become friends, and 20 years later I still love, admire, and respect him and adore his creations.

It was my job to attend all the shows, events, and functions that supported and surrounded the Fashion Week. I shared my expertise, having organized the New York shows, giving advice and suggestions on how to tighten up production elements such as the venues, lighting, and layouts. I also made suggestions on how to tame and organize the red

"Tarun has left an indelible mark on my life, my career, and my wardrobe..."

carpet arrivals, where Bollywood stars would pose every night, and, generally, gave constructive advice for making the Lakmè Fashion Week a world-class event.

I remember the wonderful times on the rooftop of the restaurant Indigo, which was only a short walk from the Taj. Here, I met designers and members of the Fashion Design Council of India (FDCI), my IMG colleagues, more fashion media, and the socialites and celebrities who wear the clothes that bring the style of Bombay to life. But I truly was not prepared for what I would see on the runways... the colours, the textiles, the embroideries, and embellishments; the easy draping of scarves in ways that only Indian women can pull off; and the gorgeous models, both men and women. The models wore exotic make-up that paired exquisitely with their dark and luscious hair, their natural curvy, sensual bodies a world away from the lean, almost anorexic, forms of the models in the US.

I was instantly hooked and in love with Indian fashion. I couldn't get enough of it. I shopped at the designers' stalls, as well as their city boutiques, which resulted in the inevitable challenge of closing the zippers on my luggage when I headed home. I could not get enough of Tahiliani's laser-printed kurtas worn over leggings. All in pinks and turquoise, embellished with jewels, pearls, and Swarovski crystals. I was so happy I was no longer head of the CFDA and did not have to wear only American designers; I could go out to galas and benefits back in New York wearing my new Indian designer clothes that no one could buy in America. Trust me, everyone asked, "Who are you wearing, and is it sold in New York?"

Tarun Tahiliani, for me, is India's Valentino with a touch of Bob Mackie thrown in for good measure. He drapes and wraps and embellishes, making every woman's dreams come true. Tahiliani's gorgeous eveningwear has made it to many CFDA Awards galas and I don't think I have ever felt more glamourous, special, or individual as when I have worn his designs. Tahiliani is a citizen of the world— the fashion education he gained in New York at Fashion Institute of Technology (FIT), whose foundation board I am a proud member of, taught him skills that he could not have learned in India. His business acumen was sharpened at the Wharton School of Business. I do not know where his talent and skills as an interior designer were honed and learned but he also has a back-up career in it if he ever needs one. His retail emporiums are as beautifully designed as his homes, which I am thrilled to have had the chance to visit and even stay in. My earlier trips to Delhi for Lakmè Fashion Week always included a dinner (a very late one) at his "farmhouse". It has always amused me that this home is called a farmhouse as it is anything but that. The lighting, candles, and trees are wrapped in jasmine and white cotton fabric, the trees smothered with little lights is a detail I will never forget and one I tried, albeit unsuccessfully, to replicate at my Hamptons home. The artwork, sculptures, books, and furniture create a home of warmth and style, a perfect backdrop for his fashion. His home in Goa, while more minimal than Delhi, is equally creative, dramatic, and inviting.

Tahiliani dresses the biggest Bollywood stars (who also happen to be his friends), Middle Eastern princesses and royalty, the crème de la crème of Indian society, and countless brides who want to feel like all of the aforementioned women on their wedding day. Tarun Tahiliani has been a part of more lavish Indian weddings than anyone can count. Here is where you will see the magic of his clothes on both men and women. The colours range from pale greys and blushes to bright pinks, greens, purples, reds, and every colour in between. The wedding ensembles take my breath away. I still do not know how Indian brides pull off wearing multiple looks and many pounds of beaded, embellished garments for several days in a row... and, oh yes, the jewellery. Nowhere on earth do you see such extraordinary necklaces, earrings, bracelets, and other ceremonial jewels encrusted with diamonds, rubies, emeralds, sapphires, and pearls. Going to a perfectly planned week-long Indian wedding needs to be on every fashion lover's bucket list. But it always comes back to the clothes. Tarun Tahiliani is the consummate Indian designer. His clothes are contemporary yet authentic Indian. He uses modern techniques combined with traditional handcrafting and textiles. Tahiliani is a proud ambassador of his country's history and culture, which is evident in his creations.

He is the godfather of the pack, making an indelible contribution to the world of fashion. Tahiliani has made a lasting impression on me and has earned a special place in my heart, my life, and my style. And for that, I will be forever grateful.

The Great Western
Hotel, Bombay in 1890.
This building became
the location of Ensemble,
the first store started by
Sal and Tarun Tahiliani,
in 1987.

INTRODUCTION

IT BEGAN IN ONE OF THE OLDEST STRUCTURES IN BOMBAY...

It began in an elegant building, one of the oldest structures in Bombay, known as the Great Western Building. The large colonial townhouse at Lion Gate had borne witness to colourful dramas since the 18th century. Originally designed as the Admiral's residence in 1764, the space has been repurposed as the Governor's bungalow; the seat of successive judicial courts; a hotel; and as a warren of rundown offices. On a cool day in December 1987, Sailaja 'Sal' and Tarun Tahiliani opened its doors to reveal Ensemble, a multi-brand fashion boutique that introduced the concept of luxury retail to the city. On the racks, along with four Indian and one American designer, was Tahiliani's label, Ahilian.

Fashion at Ensemble was more than just sharp jackets and draped dresses. The extravagance of gold and silver embroidery had broken the shackles of Nehruvian socialism. It was a world away from the tailors who called upon the houses of rich patrons with sacks of fabric on their back, which they worked upon in small workshops in the city and in far-flung villages.

"People were saying 'bye-bye khadi and hello brocade'," recalls Tahiliani.

For him, fashion was a rebellion that manifested itself in exquisite outfits that riffed on centuries-old sartorial legacies. A raw silk *kalidar* lehenga was not merely an ode to the Mughals, it allowed Tahiliani to unveil cultural histories and the Indian crafts that had been muffled as a result of colonial oppression. Though Tahiliani's creations were for the modern women of the day, his attention to

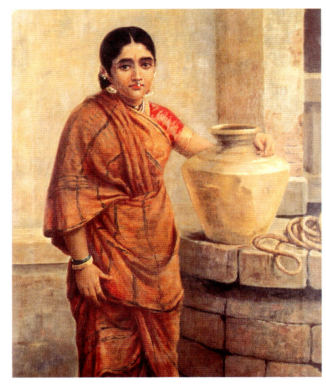

history enabled the revival of crafts that had lain dormant and brought to the fore an Indianness that was at risk of being forgotten. Tahiliani played a dual role—at once he was a couturier whose creations were the epitome of chic and a researcher who retrieved lost histories and identities. For Tahiliani, these two vocations were inextricably linked. The rediscovery of the past, to wear it on our bodies in the present, was a celebration of who we are.

The legacy of Indian fashion is greatly shaped by the changes that take place in the country. With Prime Minister Rajiv Gandhi's early reforms in the late 1980s and Prime Minister P.V. Narasimha Rao's radical liberalization policy of 1991 that opened the economy, India experienced a "second Independence". As economic transformations altered lives, an affluent society demanded unseen extravagance. Society darlings wore lace and embroidery, eyelet details and silk tulle. With collections as varied as Byzantine and Creatures of an Alien Realm, Tahiliani introduced new lines at fashion shows that were like rock concerts. At the helm of the industry, he took every opportunity, leveraging the strength of artisans, many of them tucked in nooks along Mohammed Ali Road, professionalizing them and creating an enterprise. He opened flagship stores in Bombay and Delhi, appointed young designers who had recently graduated from NIFT to his design team and gave a brand-hungry society the label culture. Tahiliani rode the wave of high growth, stepping into new markets as the first Indian designer to show in Milan and being one of the first designers to import the boning necessary in the construction of a bustier.

Changes in India wove a new sartorial expression influenced by fast fashion and the Westernization of culture. "A debate over the possible death of the sari has captured the attention of Indian fashion writers," noted the *Guardian* in 2005. Influenced by the West, yet unable to shake off the memories of his mother in resplendent saris, the Koli fisherwomen of Bombay and the traditional attires he encountered on his many journeys across rural India, Tahiliani's aesthetic remained rooted in tradition, albeit taking a detour through Europe's plunging necklines. In his journey towards a modern aesthetic, the romantic ivories in *chikankari* played with the languid minimalism of the noughties in draped jersey pieces that contained references and symbols of bygone times.

"I want to try and preserve our identity at a more cerebral level. We can't let the identity of the Indian drape get lost," he said.

Affected by the splendour of the medieval period, Tahiliani dived into history. He immersed himself in the works of Raja Ravi Varma, hypnotized by the sensuality of the beautiful women in his paintings draped in swathes of fabric. Fashion can be inspired by history while being for the now; a tribute to the past, a promise to the future. The miniatures of Bani Thani, the singer and poet from the 18th century, and her lover Raja Samanth Singh were adapted and updated to adorn a digital tee in one of Tahiliani's most iconic pieces.

One of Tahiliani's singular achievements has been the creation of the concept sari, a reinterpretation of a garment that traces its origins to the Rig Veda. His careful study of the drapes of India, the deconstruction and reconstruction of countless yards of fabric, his pilgrimage to the Mahakumbh and love for the sadhu's unfettered drape resulted in the dhoti-sari that marries Western construction with an Indian drape. Though his atelier continues to make couture for a handful of women, its presence is felt by others through a ready-to-wear line, accessories, carpets, and homes. It is a success story that baffles its founder.

"I've stood there since we opened the door to Ensemble and I've seen what it's done. I don't take credit for it all but the embroidery today is as good as that of the Mughal age. There is a celebration of beautiful Indian things. We're doing things that are more Indian," he says.

In the essays that follow, Tahiliani's role in this sartorial renaissance will be placed in historical context through the introduction of new looks and techniques that transformed the way Indian women dress. These essays cover the couture commissions, the women and men who made Tahiliani's first client list, and international popstars and society darlings. Over the course of twenty-five years, Tahiliani has transformed his business from a one-room studio in Opera House to a fashion powerhouse. The House of Tahiliani's journey is also the modern history of fashion in India and its pursuit of an idea known as India Modern.

The draped form—Past + Present = Future. India's art has rich representations of drape—from Raja Ravi Varma (1848–1906) to Jamini Roy (1887–1972). Juxtaposed with traditional examples are representations of Tahiliani's designs that show how he has been inspired by draped forms to keep them alive. Today, as women struggle with traditional drapes and styles of wearing a sari, he has developed the "structured draped form" with modern draping techniques to allow this form to pass on and not die.

ENSEMBLE
FINE CLOTHING FOR DISCERNING MEN AND WOMEN

ENSEMBLE
FINE CLOTHING FOR DISCERNING MEN AND WOMEN

ENSEMBLE
FINE CLOTHING FOR DISCERNING MEN AND WOMEN

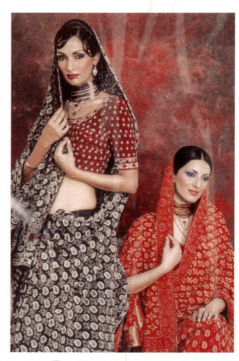

ENSEMBLE
FINE CLOTHING FOR DISCERNING MEN AND WOMEN

The Day of the
D≡SIGN≡R

Ensemble introduced a new concept in designer clothes: a platform for Indian designers to market their exclusive styles under their own labels.

SILKS AND French wine flowed with equal abundance. it was a night for stylish intoxication, the celebration of an idea whose time had come, introducing the city to a new concept in fashion retailing. Ensemble, the new designer fashion boutique at Lion's Gate was opened with the flourish and gay abandon of its creators and proprietors, 24-year-old Sailaja, 'Sal' to her friends, and Tarun Tahiliani, 25. The son of an admiral has hit upon the right fashion idea, and his wife — who displays model proportions herself and has in fact modelled for the shop's slick introductory brochure — has pitched in with elan_ At the inaugural fashion and cocktail do—very exclusive, very intimate socialites mingled with designers and models to hit the right note of success. A converted machine tools showroom, Ensemble was a dilapidated barn until interior designer Urshila Kerkar working on simple minimalist lines with wood panelling and white highlights gave it the exclusive New York-loft-look. Mannequins picked up for a song were painted bronze, and giant urns in white lent an esoteric note, creating the ideal backdrop for the glittering crowd dressed to the hilt and ready to give corn-petition to the models on the ramp. Jaya Bachchan, Devika Bhojwani, Neerjah Shah, Iama-Ii Ahluwalia whose jewellery was on sale and priced between Rs 40-Rs 200 — among the exclusive brigade, pecked gracefully at the fancy hors d'oeuvres served on stylish cane trays and sipped wine or freshly squeezed orange juice, as they awaited the main event' the exquisite outfits from Ensemble's dutch of exclusive designers.

Sailaja and Tarun Tahiliani: marketing designer styles

Finally, someone has dared to bring Indian designers out from behind dummies and drawing boards. Ensemble offers space to fashion creators who have thus far hidden behind export names and marketing labels to present their own designs under their own names. The concept, well established abroad, was obviously waiting for a bunch of gutsy kids to kick it off to a flying start here. Indian designers will finally get the limelight that is their due and a time may yet come when the Cardins and the Yves Saint Laurents will get com-petition from this part of the world. "We are the first generation of Indian designers who will be known names," says an exuberant Rohit

Khosla whose white and gold outfits—one of which was snapped up by Simple Kapadia for star sister Dimple — on display wowed the crowd even before the show started. "This wonderful outlet finally gives designers like us a chance to show Our clothes - As each collection stepped, twirled and danced its way over the wooden ramp, which has been skilfully built into the shop's design, it was obvious that this fashion vanguard had thrown itself wholeheartedly into fabric fantasies. "It has always been considered a risk to let designers do absolutely what they want," says Abu Jani who, with Sandeep Khosla, has created the imaginative Jashan collection. "But this

couple is fantastic. They let us do absolutely what we wanted and we've really gone wild with this collection."

IT WAS a fantastic flurry of finely blended Indian and Western styles that greeted the viewer (the outfits cost between Rs 2,100 and Rs 8,000) Jashan came on first with the blur of elaborate bro-cades, Benarasi silks, metallic weaves, flowing shapes and bare midriffs. Next, the only American designer, Neil Bieff, first to tap Indian crafts and skills 10 years ago, presented his really sleek couture collection, resplendent with glittering sequins and beads incorporated onto well-tailored suits, jackets and chiffon chemises—a wonderful amalgam of fantastic crafts-manship and sophisticated design. Tahiliani's own collection, Ahilian, presented a Western line of ladies' suits and coordinates adapted from fabric designs picked out of Moghul miniatures: little silk caps (Rs 300) topping off business suits; billowing rawsilks, layered tissue and organza completed the look. Then came Amaaya, the label of city designers Anita Shivdasani and Sunita Kapoor — very, very feminine, soft clothing; intricate embroidery, bead and mirror work made the traditional churidar salwar, sherwani and dhoti salwar a contemporary concept. And finally, the obvious favourite and irrepressible Rohit Khosla drew the show to a grand finale with his black-and-vibrant-colour coordinates. Khosla drew inspiration for this glittering collection from the uniforms of the President's body-guard "The colours of their medals and cummerbunds are

(continued on page 76)

FACING PAGE: "In the first years of Ensemble, as a marketing activity, we made postcards to announce new collections. These were shot against a variety of backdrops including Jehangir Sabavala's paintings and coloured *chikan* fabrics."

ABOVE: "*Bombay* magazine put Sal and me on the cover two weeks after we opened Ensemble. Photographed on December 12, the opening night. Sal is dressed in Rohit Khosla."

TT

"I want to try and preserve our identity at a more cerebral level. We can't let the identity of the Indian drape get lost."

TARUN TAHILIANI

Shyamoli Varma
photographed by
Prabuddha Dasgupta on
the terrace of Tahiliani's
home in 1989.
EARLY PRINTS & DRAPES

TT

EARLY YEARS

TARUN TAHILIANI AT THE GATES OF FASHION

Sal wearing a draped top and chiffon skirt by Ahilian. Photographed by Shantanu Sheorey for the first Ensemble catalogue.

In the photograph, the young woman is gazing at her feet, her black chiffon Ahilian skirt billows above her ankles, as if lifted by a gust of wind. The blouse flatters the slope of her shoulders, cinches her waist and then flares into full-skirted freedom. Her casual demeanour belies what this picture will come to signify in the years to come, for in that moment, the designer, the model, and the photographer are merely carrying out experimentations in style. It is not immediately apparent that this picture will find its place in the opening catalogue for Ensemble, a boutique that will transform the way Indian women dress. This image of Sailaja 'Sal' Tahiliani will leave its mark on style, heralding the arrival of Tarun Tahiliani and his quest to reshape and reclaim an Indian aesthetic.

The series of photos, shot by Shantanu Sheorey in Bombay, did not betray a sombre reality—British rule and its 150-year colonial freeze on textile crafts had suppressed Indian style. Post-Independence socialism with its ban on imports meant even buttons and zippers were hard to procure.[1] There was no fashion industry to speak of, nor was there any retail infrastructure in the 1980s. India was a sari-wearing society, a place where tailors knew little of garment construction. It was a land of exquisite textile and intricate drapes but India remained a sari-weaving society, a place where tailors knew little of garment construction.

It was in this atmosphere that Sal and Tarun Tahiliani opened the doors to a multi-brand boutique called Ensemble at Lion Gate, Bombay.

Tahiliani was at the forefront, gathering a medley of designers—Rohit Khosla, Abu Jani and Sandeep Khosla, Anuradha Mafatlal, Anita Shivdasani and Sunita Kapoor, and Niel Bieff. In a landmark move at Ensemble in 1987, the fraternity organized for the first time under one roof and heralded the beginning of the designer era in India.[2] With about 80 outfits in the open space, hanging on the racks were pieces by six designers including Tahiliani's label, Ahilian. "When we first began, I felt diffident about using my name as a brand, so we dropped the 'T' and an 'I' in my last name, which left us with 'Ahilian'. We had a name for the new label," Tahiliani shares.

On the opening night, December 12, 1987, patrons walked into a clothing store that looked like an art gallery, a store dedicated to displaying and merchandizing in a clean, modern style. As women sipped on champagne and nibbled on hors d'oeuvres, Tahiliani showed models in pencil skirts and jackets with Rs. 300 silk *topis*; in sheer *anarkalis* inspired by Mughal miniatures in silk, *jamawar*, layered tissue, organza, and lamé. "That was Bombay's first in-store fashion show and it was magical," says Shirin Mehta, a journalist who covered the opening.

A week later, Sal and Tahiliani were on the cover of *Bombay* magazine where the author noted that Ensemble was a "celebration of an idea whose time had come… a time may yet come when the Cardins and the Yves Saint Laurents will get competition from this part of the world".[3] It marked the beginning of a spare-no-expense, colour-drenched celebration of finery that took off in 1987 and has not stopped since.

—

Tarun Tahiliani was born in Bombay on July 19, 1962. The eldest of two children, his father was an admiral in the Indian Navy and his mother was one of the first female engineers in Maharashtra. Tahiliani has been sketching since his childhood. "As a child, I had to wear polio braces and had leg problems. My mother actively pushed me into art and piano lessons and encouraged my artistic inclinations even if it wasn't very common for boys to do so at the time. She exposed me to art and culture partly because I had an aptitude, but also because I could not run around like a normal child."

First, it was planes and dinghies, then as he grew older, he began sketching figures of wedding processions. "They were very detailed and accessorized," recalls Tina Tahiliani, his younger sister. Long before there was an atelier or in-house models, Tahiliani dressed Tina, seeking the finest fabrics and tailors in the city in what was an early initiation into women's fashion.

Visions of his mother in resplendent saris and her encapsulation of a modernity in the late 1960s, the habits of the nuns from his school, and the attire of Koli fisherwomen in Bombay captivated his imagination. But the world Tahiliani grew up in was heavily anglicized. "In a country that's deracinated, there is a conflict between tradition and modernity. We were Westernized, went to Jesuit schools, spoke an affected Hindi to the boys who served us at the clubs while speaking the Queen's English," he says. The interplay of East and West played an enduring role in his sartorial expression. By the time he was in high school, he won the best artist prize for a drawing of a wedding procession in which the women wore decorative saris. The words of his teacher hung in the air: "And where do you think you'll go drawing fashion models?"

As a young man, Tahiliani studied business management at Wharton School of Business in the USA, where he met Sal. Their union would electrify Indian fashion. "Ensemble was my wife Sal's idea, and it was thanks to her that I attended my first serious fashion show. We met at university studying different subjects—she pushed me to work and study and better myself." Upon his return to India in 1985, he found a country shaking off the cobwebs of socialism and trying to find its place in the world. Prime Minister Rajiv Gandhi's administration had eased some of the pinching economic restrictions on doing business and moves were made to encourage capital goods imports. Jeans were available, some houses had TVs, and with Pepsi at the corner stores,[4] the currents of globalization were being felt in India. Dissatisfied with his job of selling oil-field equipment, motivated by Sal, mentored by Rohit Khosla, and influenced by an *India Today* article titled "The Fashion Business: Looking Good", Tahiliani took a chance at fashion.

—

Tahiliani made his entry at a time when people were done with years of dreary-do. In those days, when they could barely make a sleeve in India, Tahiliani was holed up in a run-down flat on the third floor of a building in Opera House, Bombay. He sat on the ground, sketching asymmetrical kurtas, boleros, and transparent skirts with peplum tops while the tailor struggled to cut along the structured silhouette. With no mannequin and no in-house model,

Tahiliani's mother, Jaswanti Tahiliani. "I only knew modern, emancipated women, thanks to my mother. It was celebrated and normal in our Sindhi families."

Tahiliani draped on the young men who worked at Ensemble during their summer holidays. "He made the most elaborate drapes, things nobody had seen before," says Manoj Sharma, who joined as an intern in 1987. But Tahiliani lacked the practical and technical skills that went into the construction of a garment. This frustrated the perfectionist in him even though there was a great demand for his pieces.

With each drape, he played with the hemline of desire. The bewitching movements of Ahilian skirts, the elegant swirls of *anarkali*s and yards of fabric draped as sarongs enchanted the contemporary fashion set. Distinct silhouettes were emerging: structured shape with a figure-hugging drape, flowy *anarkali*s in georgettes and chiffons. On the catwalks and off, his outfits were a piece of theatre inspired by the art of the Mughal era. Much like the figures in the miniature paintings that wore fitted bodices and skirts, Tahiliani's interpretation of the outfits were cinched at the waist while transparent layers of soft muslin created a layered and textured look. Like the Mughals, Tahiliani seldom sent out his models without *bajuband*s that were adorned with precious stone and created what was known as the 'TT look'.

Tahiliani's move into an empty board room above Ensemble at the Great Western Building saw people knocking at his door. First to join the studio were students from fashion schools across the country and, soon enough, sensing the excitement of the place, his auditor Ratna Vyas quit her full-time job at the time and joined Tahiliani's team as a financial officer. They worked crammed at one big table—some sketched, others coloured in the ornate embroidery; there was a sense of possibility. "There was a buzz because we were doing something nobody had done before," recalls Anupama Kabra, who wrote part of her thesis on his first collection that was shown abroad.

—

Tahiliani's collections were modern yet Indian. He fashioned a skirt from black and white Benarasi fabric, and clubbed soft *mal anarkali*s with little jackets and wide lapel kurtas nipped at the waist with billowing salwar pants. His connection with textile designer Asha Sarabhai and hers with Japanese fashion designer Issey Miyake imprinted on Tahiliani the value of finishing, and their connect of modernity with tradition fascinated him. With each line, there were greater Indian influences where even pin tucks incorporated *kangri jali* detail. Inspired by the art of Jehangir Sabavala and his cubist style, the Fields of India Collection in 1991 saw Tahiliani experiment with angular geometry on blouses and saris in rust and electric blue. The images were shot against a hand-painted backdrop in tribute to Sabavala. From there to Bhagalpur, the small town in Bihar that inspired a big collection, he made bolder forays into Indian silhouettes, from *anarkali*s to drop-waist empire lines in jewel tones.

His small studio was a departure from the fabric world where tailors and seamstresses visited houses with piles of books on fashion and patterns and attempted to put together Western-inspired outfits. Tahiliani's work was a shift from the shapeless salwar-suit and the oft-found dowdy prints in haphazard colours. Ahilian pieces were in muted tones, devoid of the heavy gold embroidery that symbolized luxury. More than any other designer, he was responsible for the shift away from textile shops.

Tahiliani's designs came at a time when India was undergoing a revival in the arts in all forms of expression, from poetry to theatre. "Very early on, I asked what my role would be, and I realized it would be the preservation of culture," he says.

He dug deep into history to find inspiration. His careful study of Mughal and Rajput miniature art reflected a particular Indianness in his work, but his structured designs were a break away from tradition. According to Tahiliani, fashion is enriched by paying respect to the past but thrives when updated to suit changing realities. His search for the past in costumes inspired by the Peshwas or aristocratic robes from the Mughal era revealed a creative reinterpretation of historical styles, an evolution of design rather than a copy.

For him, garments could revive a broken history. "Ravi Varma was the first Indian painter who documented realism but everyone wore saris, and Indian fashion didn't change. Georgian, Edwardian, the Dandy, or the 1920s, '30s, '50s—in the West, fashion changed decade on decade. India remained the same. It was a textile industry in a textile world."

—

Tahiliani worked like an architect of fashion. His sketches were ingeniously conceived where yards of fabric spiralled around the body to form both bodice and skirt. Almost sculptural in his approach, his idea was to mould without clinging. However, he lacked skilled technicians despite the presence of an army of tailors adept at hand-sewing until he met Ajju in Bapa Dhragendra's fashion design company. Arjun "Ajju" Godiya was an exceptional hand at cutting

patterns and a wizard at sewing these with hidden seams, using nips, and tucks to maximum effect.

It was the summer of 1987 when Tahiliani passed over a sketch to the young tailor who meticulously recreated the toiles by draping it on his own body at a time when there were no dress forms. He did not stop until it cinched perfectly. This piece was a precursor to the modern concept sari which would see several reincarnations at the House of Tahiliani, beginning from a drape on a pencil skirt to a draped dhoti. Stylistically, these pieces were so complex that it was difficult to figure out how to wear them but they were light to the touch and felt like liquid silk upon wearing.

Technically, however, Tahiliani was grappling with sizing. In one of the earlier shoots with model Mehr Jesia, where she is seen laughing, posing without artifice, the campaign was a naturalistic portrait. Though the dress, with a quilted under base and fluting, looked beautiful, it could not be produced again or fit against measurements accurately. This process of trial and error frustrated Tahiliani. He decided to make India's first detailed sizing chart.

Hurdles aside, the early shoots were spontaneous, almost like improvized adventures that used Bombay as their set. Under the arches of the Gateway of India, Jesia was photographed in a sari with an organza drape and machine-embroidered blouse from the Fields of India Collection. The piece was finished with a textured shawl and a choker. In another image on his rooftop where the minaret of the Taj Mahal Palace hotel peeped in, Shyamoli Varma was captured in a jacquard wrap skirt with a blouse at a time when models did their own makeup and were styled by the designers themselves. In the early years of Ensemble and Ahilian, photographers like Prabuddha Dasgupta and Shantanu Sheorey were commissioned to do most of the shoots. Both photographers went on to become icons in the world of fashion photography. Tahiliani prioritized personality over polish. He allowed the model to have a say over how she was portrayed. "There was no posturing," says Jesia. If it wasn't art, it was an honest document of its time. "If you ever wore a Tarun choli, you knew you were in a new fit. This was very different from what the choli *darzi*s made; it had darts, a corseted quilted look. It was so different from what anyone had seen," recalls an early client.

These early experimentations fed into the age of the fashion show. Tahiliani opened the shows and Rohit Khosla closed them to much critical acclaim. The images of Mehr Jesia and Shyamoli Varma went on to launch the careers of the models and photographers. Soon supermodels ruled the scene while many of the future Miss World and Miss Universe contestants started their careers on these catwalks.

—

OUR INDIAN style was always timeless. Evolving through the millenium. Do we need fashion as a western construct?

TARUN TAHILIANI

An outfit was an invitation to a larger question. What does it mean to be Indian? What does that look like? Textiles and design have long played a part in defining India's cultural identity but what does that mean in a rapidly modernizing environment? He sought an answer to that question when he took off on a long drive across Kutch, Gujarat, with a book by Martand Singh on the Vishwakarma exhibitions.

Tahiliani's clothes were to be answers to the questions preying on his mind. Rather than only the "identity of self", the design studio would also look at the "identity of a place"; the crucial question would not be "who am I?" but "where is here?" In his travels across villages and towns, he came across statuesque men whose white dhotis had been coloured by the sand, women in 20-metre lehengas, their dupattas surging in the wind. At a store, he stood hypnotized by an old woman with nine earrings in each ear and sporting Ray-Bans. "In their sameness, they were fiercely different. It was the opposite of cloning," he recalls.

On the night of his first fashion show at the Taj Mahal Palace Hotel in Bombay, Varma appeared on the raised catwalk, a vision in a sheer lehenga with a peplum top and a *mala* of flowers draped on her arm. When the power went out, Jesia insisted she would still walk and emerged in the dark room,

devoid of music, where the only sound was the melody of the *ghunghrus* on the lehenga. It was a small dose of magic, of being transported to a place of real wonder. The clothes, the shows, harnessed a sense of possibility.

Tahiliani was fascinated by fashion as a cultural, historical, social, and political phenomenon affected by histories of colonialism, and the processes of decolonization and globalization. Free from commercial constraints and demands of clients, he approached fashion in a manner one approaches literature, a subject that ought to be studied. It was then that Tahiliani enrolled at Fashion Institute of Technology in New York. That gruelling year in 1990 and the hours spent in the construction of jackets, skirts, and drapes invigorated Tahiliani.

—

After a couple of years of shuttling between the US and India, Tahiliani had a recurring dream of India, of peacocks and palaces. He packed his bags and returned. He moved his studio from Bombay to Delhi and settled into an urban village. "Perhaps unbeknown to me, there was this influence of India that was so sensual and so beautiful and true to my heart," he says. He had come home for a second act.

An oil painting by Tahiliani, 1987. "While I was not trained as an artist, I am influenced by the artist Anjolie Ela Menon, who had a studio in my parents' garage in the early years of her career. I love the effects of dribbling down and the use of turpentine and linseed oil; they eat into the paint, creating very interesting webs."

"When you fly over India, you see tiny mosaics of fields. I named the collection 'Fields of India' and used geometric patterns that evoke the spliced colour of Indian fields from the air. You can see these on the blouse that the model is wearing, and other graphic renditions, which were explored in print and multicolour. We asked billboard artists to create a backdrop based on Jehangir Sabavala's cubist landscapes using graphics and colours similar to the cubist fields and hills of India. This provided the perfect context to the collection that included *jamawar* prints and weaves from the south."
FIELDS OF INDIA, 1992

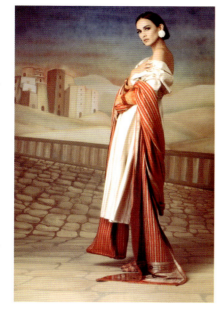

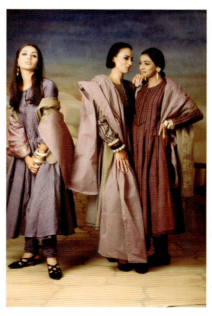

FACING PAGE: Shyamoli Varma in a draped surplice kurta, using an antique cummerbund as a stole.

ABOVE: These photographs were taken by another giant of fashion photography, Ashok Salian.

Mehr Jesia in an empire draped dress that uses fluting, draping, and fringing. This marked the beginning of structured drapes in Tahiliani's work.

"MEHR JESIA BROUGHT ALL OUR EARLY FASHION TO LIFE & VITALITY— MUSE + TEACHER."

TARUN TAHILIANI

FACING PAGE: Mehr Jesia in a Swarovski mesh bodice with a chiffon anklet sari, 1999/2000. "Thanks to Isabella Blow, I had begun a collaboration with Swarovski, who were attempting to make inroads into India. The mesh was something that we used over a skin lining to give the illusion of a tattoo with tiny crystals, and we paired this with shorts and an ankle-length sari—so it appeared to be a half dress and half sari."

*"Fashion is alive when paying homage
to the past and yet lives & gains life
from or in the moment."*

TARUN TAHILIANI

Tahiliani's first solo
show, titled the
Rubaiyat, was held at
the Dorchester Hotel,
London, in 1994.

TT

NEW LINES · NEW TECHNIQUES

DRAPE, CRAFTS AND CONSTRUCTION TECHNIQUES SYNTHESIZED

In September 1994, Tarun Tahiliani's first solo show opened at the Dorchester Hotel in London. Titled the Rubaiyat, inspired by Persian poet Omar Khayyam's Sufi verses on love and righteousness, the Autumn/Winter 1994 Collection embodied the guiding spirit of the fashion house: to adapt from the past and become of the present. Models walked in flared *kalidar* kurtas, in designs that concealed more than they revealed, made of delicate chiffon and organza, topped with structured jackets. Each piece was hand-drawn, every detail hand-rendered and tailored at a time when there was not even a computer in Tahiliani's Bombay studio.

The ballroom at the Dorchester buzzed with nervous excitement as Tahiliani revealed not one but six collections in his debut. The Mughal Collection was a study in detail, its patina of dusty pale colours inspired from carpets. Islamic embroidery—flowy and floral with *zardozi*, French knots and flat *ari* stitches—created shadows, while textures added depth. The Byzantine line explored geometricism, using chunky cabochon stones framed by pearls with gold and glitter thrown in on bodices. Creatures of an Alien Realm was an antithesis of the previous two and presented graphic

hand-painted coordinates inspired by wrought iron. It was unlike any other sartorial expression the West had seen from the subcontinent, and the theatrical thread holding the lines together was India itself. The Rubaiyat catered to every taste, every body, and every pocket. Save for one, all the pieces from the six lines were sold.[1]

Watching from the front row was Isabella Blow, a British fashion editor, aesthete, and talent-spotter, who would later declare Tahiliani the "Karl Lagerfeld of India". Through this collection, the "Made in India" tag acquired a new meaning and the fledgling Ahilian label was replaced by a new one— Tarun Tahiliani. Tahiliani's next step was to move his studio from the environs around the Taj Mahal Palace in South Bombay to an urban village in Delhi in 1995.

—

Delhi was more consistent with Tahiliani's vision of India; from its small villages to its proximity to the craft belt, the capital held an enduring lure. An enthusiastic press ran stories of his move as Tahiliani settled into a studio down

45

In 1995 Tahiliani moved to Delhi, a city he associated with "Mughals and medieval magic, peacocks, majestic monuments, the passion of the northern plains and heat and dust." Delhi had a profound influence on his work. In this painting, "Rotations", artist Ravinder Dutt shows a Mughal emperor flying above the imperial city in a peacock chariot. Tahiliani's sister commissioned the artist to impose his face to depict him as the Mughal emperor.

46

a rubble road in Chirag Dilli where a sizeable community of migrant workers in the garment trade resided.[2] With its six tailors and four-member design team, the studio stood past the oldest living *khirni* tree in the city, rising from the shrine of a 14th-century Sufi saint. Chirag Dilli, much like Delhi itself, underwent many reincarnations, notable among them was the resettlement of Punjabi refugees whose presence had a profound impact on Tahiliani's style, reflected in pieces that were far more glamourous than Bombay's understated elegance. "There is always a sociological basis to clothes," says Tahiliani.

For him, the charm of engaging with the day-to-day affairs of the locality, where women in saris and salwar-suits went from door to door selling their wares, calling out their services, was precious. "In these villages, before television made us so homogeneous, everyone wore Indian clothes," he says. Tahiliani was driven by the belief that fashion and clothing influence articulations of the body and self and can define experiences of any time and place. To him, the everyday woman and her aesthetic were a window to a country as it modernized, through them he studied the evolving aspirations and sensibilities of the transforming India. Subsequently, with each collection—from Fluted, for which Tahiliani draped hundreds of metres of red fabric beneath the crystal chandeliers of the ballroom at the Taj Palace in Delhi, to the screen-printed line that was the precursor to digital printing and a harmonious collaboration between art and fashion—Tahiliani commented on his vision of India.

Delhi also gave him a bigger canvas with the presence of strong summers and biting winters. The studio had a plethora of fabrics to experiment with—lawn, weightless *malmal*, denser charmeuse, and velvet—all made an appearance in his pieces. Tahiliani's love for silk wools and knits was seen in the Hakoba Collection, which introduced mechanized eyelet work, a new technique that exemplified one of the early uses of technology. It mimicked the delicate Lucknowi (or Lakhnavi) *chikankari* and was run on *mal*, organza, silk, and raw silk until he began working with a *chikankari* embroiderer. Soon, *chikankari* became a mainstay of the house. Delhi's proximity to the traditional enclaves of craftspeople in the cities of Bareilly, Jaipur, and Lucknow meant that Tahiliani had access to many kinds of artisans. British colonial rule had aggressively promoted machine-made foreign products in India, in the process destroying the country's traditional handicrafts known the world over for their artistry, to create a market for British products. Tahiliani attempted to undo years of dependency on machine-made clothes with a focus on *chikankari*, playing a part in the revival of the craft.

As Tahiliani's collections became season-specific, each season produced a spectacle, an introduction to techniques both novel and forgotten. In the Jewel line, inspired by Cartier,

FACING PAGE: The Rubaiyat Collection of 1994 embodies the DNA of the Tahiliani brand: adapt from the past and become of the present. Here, Mehr Jesia wears the concentric thread sherwani with perma pleated pants. The collection was a nod to women taking all forms of male dress in their self-expression—an adaptation to the present.

ABOVE: A sari blouse from the Rubaiyat Collection with clusters of semi-precious stones (garnet, lapis, jade and cornelian) in the traditional fruit formation seen in old classic Indian artworks.

necklace designs from a coffee-table book were imprinted on the borders of shaded saris. Fluting and draping evolved as the design house innovated with each line, propelling the fashion world into a permanent state of flux. Industries of the fine crafts—*gotta* from Hyderabad, *baadla* and *chikan* from Lucknow, *chanderi* from Maheshwar, *patola* from Gujarat, brocade from Benaras, *kanjivaram* from the South—were revitalized, with an emphasis on the customization of fabric into garments. The aim was to make something new out of old techniques. As the development of silhouettes was introduced and refined each season, Tahiliani remained committed to draping that reached new heights with the Fluted Collection.

One person played a role of cardinal importance in Tahiliani's stylistic evolution—Minal Modi. A Bombay socialite, Modi entered Tahiliani's life at the time of Tanya Godrej's wedding in 1997, and her couture request to be "wrapped like a turban" would have an enduring impact upon Tahiliani. Draping on her body, as opposed to a mannequin, was a sophistication Tahiliani repeated many times subsequently; it allowed a kind of exoticism that would guide Tahiliani's drape-and-shape legacy. Modi's formidable character, flair, and access to the finest materials from London to Milan ensured that her influence spread beyond the requirements of a couture commission. Modi was style personified as she appeared in the atelier with her magnificent collection of pieces—corsets from Vera Wang to Vivienne Westwood—that few had seen before. One piece, a Vivienne Westwood corset with a drape, preoccupied the studio for weeks, at the end of which Tahiliani and Ajju, the head of tailoring, produced the Fluted Collection for their first show in Delhi. Through the show stalked haute couture visions, models wrapped in soft and graceful georgette and chiffon, in a palette of strong colours. The effect was in part Grecian, in part Madame Grès. The underlying theme was a romantic modernity with an illusion that they were wrapped in fabric, but the layers had been constructed around a corset. The muse at the heart of this show and many others to come was Modi, who lent her inimitable touch of magic to the modern image of India that Tahiliani sought to create.

—

In the Apsara Collection (1996), depicting courtesans from the court of Lord Indra, Tahiliani celebrated sensuality and desire as models walked down the ramp in beaded halter bustiers, with strings of pearls cascading down to their navel while a drape secured their modesty. Lakhsmi Rana who walked as an *apsara* recalls the moment as a "fantasy" and a tribute not simply to celestial nymphs but also to dusky women in a society obsessed with skin colour.

Tahiliani's repertoire varied from one fashion cycle to the next, veering towards hedonism as he sent out models in crinkle, in textured skirts cut on a bias paired with quilted bralettes and strings of rhinestones adorning the neck. Having experienced significant growth since his arrival in Delhi, Tahiliani moved his studio to Mehrauli. Adjacent to the Qutub complex, Mehrauli is embedded in the historic map of the capital; the Qutub Minar is a defining silhouette of Delhi.

The Mughal period was an essential reference for the house in the absence of a modern fashion history beyond the sartorial influences of the British Raj on Indian costume.[3] Tahiliani found inspiration from Mughal miniatures that documented Empress Noor Jahan's love for intricate embroidery; the use of *chikankari* as the symbol of nobility in Emperor Jahangir's court; and the delicate floral motifs of Lucknowi artisans. For Tahiliani, the miniatures were capsules of romance, history, and folklore, with their gold-tinted Persian lettering against backdrops of royal blue, rich burgundy, and verdant green, colours that also made an appearance in his pieces.

Much like the Mughal era, when fashion and architecture were connected, when motifs that were seen on royal textiles were the same as those on monuments, his lehengas too were embellished with rhinestones, Swarovski crystals, and beading based on the designs of ornate trellises. Notable was his Padshahnama Collection that was true to the miniature paintings, with fine detailed embroidery where each *khakha* took days to make. Subdued yet extravagant, it was a grand departure from the glam and glitz of the Tahiliani brand. He also now had a team of in-house embroiderers, which made him better able to control quality and protect designs under the weak intellectual property laws of the country.

—

Despite the transformations in the industry, the government viewed Indian fashion as being inextricably linked with Indian textiles while the business of fashion was considered an extension of traditional textile-weaving and embroidery. High fashion was not valued as a new industry but merely as a positive force for reviving old ones. Therefore, when the National Institute of Fashion Technology (NIFT) was formalized in 1986 and operated from a shopping arcade

in New Delhi's Samrat Hotel, it was viewed as a solution to an export conundrum. In 1991–92, India's exports of readymade garments reached Rs. 6,282 crores, almost double of the 1989–90 numbers.[4] Over the next decade, exports multiplied but the country's garments were viewed as tacky and low-end. Through NIFT, the government hoped to alter these perceptions.[5] For Tahiliani, NIFT was something else altogether. In NIFT Delhi, he found a pool of talented young designers who were formally trained in India. When Gautam Rakha, a NIFT graduate, joined his team, a path was paved for partnerships between young designers and the House of Tahiliani. The results were electric pieces like a blue and gold "Bangkok lehenga" inspired by the temples of Bangkok, a stretch embossed velvet-lycra halter blouse with a jewelled collar teamed with a tulle sari, and saris with cut dana jaals in a step away from the traditional dabka and zardozi. "Tarun always encouraged us to express ourselves, he never held us back," says Rakha of his early years with the fashion house.

Fashion possesses the power to reflect life. Tahiliani bridged the gap between past and present through "fusion". By the 1990s, more and more Indian women wore Western fashion and for his 1999 couture show in Delhi, Tahiliani presented a collection for "the completely modern woman in touch with her roots", notes an India Today article. On the catwalk were models in sheer saris worn over figure-hugging velvet petticoats while a high-yoked evening gown with an attached pallu wrapped over bare shoulders was a seamless merger of the East and West. "Indians rich and poor live swathed in silk or pure cotton and surrounded by the finest textiles made by handloom. Yet all this wealth of fabric, often enhanced by lavish embroideries or skilful appliqués, somehow never finds its way into international fashion, unless shaped by designers from abroad, who have recently become fascinated by saris and Indian fabrics," observed the New York Times in 1989.[6]

In a bid to boost fashion's profile, Tahiliani and six other designers and a businessman came together to form the Fashion Design Council of India (FDCI) in 1999. Founded to represent the interests of fashion designers in India and nurture the growth of the industry, the FDCI would also act as a platform that lobbied for the rights of designers with the government and be a mouthpiece for the fashion industry. One of its first decisions was to instate a Fashion Week along the lines of the Fashion Weeks in Paris, which would be not simply a glamourous spectacle but also a trade show.

Meanwhile, Tahiliani was carving a new path: his clothes were on the racks at renowned boutiques, from Joseph in London and Eleonora in Rome to Scoop in New York. Each collection sold faster than the previous as elegant women from around the globe flocked to the new studio in Mehrauli. It was here that Tahiliani started digital printing, overlaying actual images with virtual versions. In a fashion house known for its handwork, digital technique introduced an element of technological wizardry, resulting in one of the most iconic looks of the house—the jewelled tee. Tucked away in Gurgaon, he came across a printer who was able to print on fabric in a way not seen before in India. Tahiliani picked jewellery motifs from a book called the Crown Jewels—emeralds, rubies, diamonds—and overlaid images of the Nizam's jewels in striking collages accentuated with lace and pearls. Depth was added by incorporating images from another volume, Romance of the Cashmere Shawls. Abstractions aside, illustrations of the collage were done on the figure so that the pattern connected with the body. Among the first pieces produced with this amalgamation of inspirations were the pearl robes and, soon after, the jewelled tee. With Modi in the studio, they created ruched tops, which left one guessing: Is it a T-shirt or is it a choli?

As Tahiliani's star rose, so did recognition from places overseas. This notably came in the form of an invitation to show at Milan's 2004 Spring/Summer Fashion Week. He would be the first Indian designer to show at Milan. His aesthetic was already headed in that direction, with leaner cuts and precise tailoring refreshed by new techniques. The studio busied itself in creating a line that was modern yet rooted in India. The result was jewelled tees with the portrait of a Rajput princess that brought together new printing with machine embroidery in gold. Chikankari turned graphic and was combined with sequins and embroidery. However, when Tahiliani went for a recce to Milan, he called the studio, announcing he would have to sketch the pieces all over again. His necklines were far too high. Italian fashion editors were pushing Tahiliani to drop the neckline, which would alter the proportions entirely. The outcome—a chikan tunic with a plunging thirteen-inch neckline paired with chikankari cigarette pants debuted on that catwalk.

"Nobody thought you could do that with chikan," recalled Aseem Kapoor, a NIFT graduate who witnessed Tahiliani push himself to the furthest reaches of creativity. The remainder of the collection, from the corset with spare embroidery on model Bhawna Sharma to the palazzo pants,

In the age of the "bandage" dress, Tahiliani began making its own "bandages" that were held together by Swarovski cup chains and jewels. This was a nod to India's past—jewels adorning the body in the most astonishing ways. The sculpture is a reflection of what Tahiliani imbibed growing up and the sari blouse and drape on the model (*facing page*) is his interpretation.

was a virtual treatise on artisanal skills that illustrated Tahiliani's sensitivity to history coupled with a belief in the idea of a modern India. Despite the Italian influence, India remained front and centre as Tahiliani flew eighteen models and the hair-and-makeup team from India. The show started with Mehr Jesia in a couture sari and reached its crescendo to classical music, a harmonious mix of Nusrat Fateh Ali Khan and Luciano Pavarotti. Three brides in lehengas closed the show and applauding from the front row was Minal Modi.

"It was the beginning of a new era," recalls Sharma, who walked for Tahiliani for years to come.

Milan gave Tahiliani the opportunity to dive into what he loved most: luxury *prêt*. It heralded the beginning of his ready-to-wear line as the design team focused on precision-cutting and tailoring. Pattern making was given prominence and how pieces are to be proportioned occupied the studio, providing a cleaner vision for ready-to-wear. Lighter embroideries replaced the heavy *zardozi* to suit international clients at a time when Japanese minimalism dominated *prêt*. Orders came from Tokyo, Dubai, and Rome for digitally printed tees, pencil skirts, and *chikankari* tunics as the clothes became less fussy while Tahiliani played with separates and collages. Meanwhile, Aseem Kapoor began work on a menswear *prêt* line that included jodhpur pants and linen *bundi*s, first shown in 2005 when Katrina Kaif came riding atop an elephant. The buzz around Tahiliani's menswear kept growing too as he showed men in drapes in ivory, beige, and black at the Men's Fashion Week in New Delhi in 2010. Stylistically, these years heralded a new chapter in Tahiliani's style that had matured over the years and was nourished by a touch that was utterly modern.

JEWELLED CLASPS

The use of jewels became a signature of Tarun Tahiliani's designs. Jewels are cast as clasps, closures and *bajubandh*s akin to the Greek Doric chiton (a single piece of fabric draped and fastened at the shoulder using a pin) and evolved into becoming full bodices.

CHIKANKARI

Chikankari, a traditional embroidery style from Lucknow, saw a great revival thanks to the efforts of SEWA, an organization that brought together *chikan* artisans (mostly women) in 1984, and other designers adopting it for their designs. Tahiliani calls *chikankari* "the Indian lace" and "finds it incredible in the way it moulds itself to the body". He has used *chikankari* extensively both in traditional designs as well as modern impressions.

According to him this adaptation of a traditional form to modern design is "the real way to keep our crafts alive". TOP LEFT: Deepika Padukone wearing a sari with tiny insets of Swarovski crystals; TOP RIGHT: The more traditional blouses, form-fitted kurtas with a salwar. BOTTOM LEFT AND RIGHT: Various avatars of how *chikankari* has been used in Tahiliani designs. FACING PAGE: Tailored corset with a slim, long kickout skirt.

Mehr Jesia wears a long
slip georgette dress that
has traditional elements
of various *chikankari*
stitches—*phool*, the
ghaas patti, the *phal*,
and traditional blocks
done in an art nouveau
patternation.

MILAN

Spring/Summer 2002

"Although a lot of these experiments in the mounting wave were already happening, it was going to Milan that really fast forwarded a certain kind of modernity. My friend, the fashion designer, Peachoo Datwani told me that in Europe they do not appreciate things being embroidered from head to toe. They would much rather see an artwork because it feels special, unlike the Indian way of seeing everything clustered from A to Z. At the conference in Milan, the press looked at the clothes and said Italian women need their clothes to be sexier. So, they literally took a pair of scissors and forced the neck lines down to 11-12 inches, almost down to the waist! On our return to India, we began to apply this to our clothes. We used ideas such as adding bits of sequins; using belts, which I have always loved on a *kurti* with a short skirt; a long jacket with drape and pencil trousers. We applied traditional techniques to contemporary silhouettes and this defined the studio at this point. The buckles for this collection (*facing page and following pages*) used to hitch A-line skirts and the *kurtis,* were made by my friend Viren Bhagat, the renowned jeweller. These are exquisite pieces slung together with a little *potli.* I love the juxtaposition of the buckle's casual ease along with the superb quality of *chikankari.*"

"The *chikan* tunic was made when we started doing plunging necklines and combining *chikan* with sequins. This is worn with a short A-line skirt that is then hitched by a simple belt that had the buckle designed by Viren Bhagat and slung together with a little *potli*."
SPRING/SUMMER 2002

"My dear friend Viren Bhagat, the finest jeweller, made these bidri buckles for me. I've called him 'Modern Mughal' ever since."

TARUN TAHILIANI

A chiffon kaftan, hitched up and clinched with a quilted corset lacing at the back.
SPRING/SUMMER 2002

"It was the commencement of a fresh chapter in Indian prêt. All of a sudden, familiar cultural icons, techniques were being juxtaposed in an entirely unconventional manner. It had a sense of familiarity, yet it exuded a distinct modernity, reflecting NOW!"

BHAWNA SHARMA

In the Spring/Summer 2002 show, for the first time, Tahiliani showed special digital printing of Indian miniatures and patterns on surfaces that were embellished with Swarovski components and pearls and crystals to bring the jewels to life. These were paired with big hipster belts and trousers, quilted bomber jackets, hip yokes, and big skirts. Tahiliani recalls, "The east-west of tribal India and miniature paintings just fused in to one kind of expression, which would describe the collages that we all had in our heads with the way we had been brought up. This began to define a new movement."

FACING PAGE: Nizam Golconda necklace tees with cargo harem pants. SPRING/SUMMER 2002

FOLLOWING PAGES: The well-known jewel-tone T-shirts inspired by some of the Nizami necklaces and embellished with soldered Swarovski jewel elements. This show forced Tahiliani to take the big leap forward in terms of his "India Modern" sensibility.

A *bandhani ajrak* sari with a crinkle crêpe skirt and a satin-draped corset blouse.
AUTUMN/WINTER 2013

06

DON'T TUCK THE SARI IN

On day two of the Wills India Fashion Week, Tarun Tahiliani was backstage fixing a drape on a concept sari in indigo *bandhani* and *ajrak*. The teal blue of the sari was a slice of the Allahabad night sky under which millions gathered for the Mahakumbh, the pilgrimage that had inspired the Autumn/Winter 2013 Kumbhback Collection. It was an audacious attempt at the impossible: to capture the banks of the Ganga with its sadhus atop silver chariots, the ascetic *naga*s, smeared only in ash, mystics in shades of crimson, and a flood of men and women in a medley of colours onto a piece of cloth.

The drapery of the holy men and women—the casual magic of a whirl across the hips and a swirl at the back—had a purity that the design team sought to imbibe. Rohit Chawla's photography—of men with matted dreadlocks and necklaces of beads and marigolds—was pinned on the mood board in Tahiliani's sprawling Gurgaon atelier. By

draping, pleating, ruching and otherwise swathing bodies in fabric based on the styles of the sadhus, they attempted to add the elusive ingredient in the house's signature look—India Modern.

The serenity of the indigo sari, the image of beautiful women on the ramp hid the painstaking journey behind it. Tahiliani's sketches with layers upon layers to reinforce the sadhu's complex drape required a mixture of textures that Aseem Kapoor and he found at a crafts exhibition. *Ajrak*, in their first few samples, was paired with a *bandhani* sari, and senior designer Pooja Haldar amalgamated the two to create a sumptuous drape that traced the body's contours. On top was the coy femininity of a Victorian corset built under looser draperies. It was of then and now, of here and there—the Tahiliani way—and the piece crystallized the quintessential "TT woman".

In 1643, a young man called Jinda Jiva Khatri migrated from Sindh to Kutch with the craft of his father: *ajrak* hand-block printing using natural dyes. The Khatri family settled in Dhamadka, a village on the banks of the river Saran where they washed the fabric, colouring the water red from madder root, black from iron rust, and a vibrant yellow from pomegranate skin. So well regarded was their craft that the king of the erstwhile Cutch state (now Kutch, a part of Gujarat) patronized it. He bolstered the artisanal community by inviting embroiders from Iran and Afghanistan, and *bandhani* artisans from Sindh, and soon the little patch of desert was transformed into a thriving cottage industry. Upon the arrival of Europeans the Khatri family traded with the Portuguese and Dutch and life was good until Europe's industrialization in the 17th century brought a change in fortunes. As synthetic dyes from France entered the market, *ajrak* teetered on the brink of becoming a lost art.

When the first ships set sail from Europe for the subcontinent, they sought spices, but it was textiles that dominated their imports.[1] So immense was the "Indian craze" for textiles in French society that the French government had to ban its import in 1685.[2] Indian calico, muslin prints, *toiles peintes*, and chintz were available on the thriving black market. Sensing an economic opportunity, the French monarchy reversed the ban, allowing imports, and encouraged French manufacturers to imitate Indian fabrics. Despite their best attempts, the French factories could not match India's weaves or the long-lasting dyes until Christophe Philippe Oberkampf, a manufacturer born into a family of dyers, made a few changes. Oberkampf shifted production from small-scale manufacturing to large factories[3] and worked tirelessly with scientists, seeking the best synthetic dyes to match the vibrant colours of India. Crucially, he tied up with a popular French artist, Jean-Baptiste Huet, and made prints that referenced events of the day, from the first hot-air balloon flight in 1783 to Napoleon's invasion of Egypt in 1798.[4] With a desire to remain on top of events, high society had fallen for not just French fashion but also for the idea that fashion can reflect social and political change.

Thus, the origins of the modern fashion system, with its "seasons" of trends, was conceived in response to France's answer to Indian cloth.

If the pantsuit is the symbol of modernity, the House of Tahiliani took a great leap forward in 2003. In response to not too many young women being used to wearing saris, Tahiliani developed multiple variations of what he called the "concept sari". These saris afforded the freedom of a Western dress—it had a loosely attached drape and a separate choli, just as one would wear in the sari, but here the petticoat and the drape were combined. In a first for Indian fashion, the design house had been invited to show at Milan for the 2004 Spring/Summer Fashion Week. The Indian fashion industry was at something of a crossroads. Long dominated by the sari and the lehenga, led by an insatiable demand for opulent embroidery, India's fashion elite had shown itself to prefer a "Made in Italy" suit over an Indian tailored Western outfit. Now, the Italians wanted to know what a transforming India had to offer. Meetings were held between Tahiliani and his counterparts in an initiative led by the Indo–Italian Chamber of Commerce. They proposed a corporeal, powerful ideal of female sexuality. Tahiliani knew some major changes would need to happen. "They were pushing us towards a new idea and it was inevitable. All Indian designers had to make the silhouette more contemporary," says Tahiliani.

Even before Tahiliani picked up his pencil to sketch for Milan, Kapoor recalls that Tahiliani had never sketched the "safe-seven neckline of India". His proportions were always made true to Milan and then yanked up to suit India. But now, with one alteration, all the proportions changed. Although Tahiliani's style often had historic origins, updating the look with an undercurrent of modernity and sexuality was the need of the hour. A balance between the two was seen in the digitally printed jewelled tee in a new look. Working with a printer in Gurgaon, Tahiliani merged the motifs of England's crown jewels with the Nizam's jewels and the printer transformed them into richly coloured digital prints on minis and boleros. On a T-shirt was the bejewelled bust of the 18th-century singer and poet Bani Thani, often referred to as the Mona Lisa of India. A jacket was adorned with the face of her Rajput lover, King Sawant Singh, with Swarovski crystals and pearls around the nape of the neck.

From a digitally printed tunic to a corset with a drape and Swarovski crystals on *chikankari*, this was hybrid fashion at its finest. There was an appliqué *kurti* with a skirt and

Neha in glam goddess mode—once again a trellis corset with a fluted bodice, worn with a big voluminous draped and panelled skirt—this was the first show where again draping and tribal influences were in sync.
SPRING/SUMMER 2008

> *"Fashion as a Western construct didn't exist in India in the 1980s. The sari has always been there. If I parachuted down then, I would know which part of the country I was in from the way people draped themselves, the textiles they wore, but today, India is becoming generic."*

TARUN TAHILIANI

an embroidered waist belt, *kurti*s paired with jodhpurs made in stretch gabardines. Corsetry, which was done in couture, was introduced in ready-to-wear. The shining star of the evening in Milan was a glorious *chikan* pantsuit, with a thirteen-inch plunge neckline and *chikan* cigarette pants that illustrated a mastery over cut, fit, and embroidery. It was from this moment onwards that Tahiliani turned his focus to *prêt-à-porter*, his true passion.

—

Fashion is the darling of capitalism, able to express itself in social life like no other phenomenon. As India awakened from its socialist slumber and marched into the 1990s with economic reforms, a golden cycle of high growth rates was set into motion. During India's wonder years, Tahiliani created clothes—a one shoulder drape with a shoulder pad; laser-cut corset belts in heavy leather; a Grecian drape; a folded drape on a bias, *chikankari* on a viscose jersey, on net; a sari-inspired drape in very fine cotton; digital printing with hand-cut lace patches in a tribute to Alexander McQueen; animal prints from printmakers in the West, reminiscent of Cavalli; a biker jacket on a lace kurta; tattooed stockings in *jamawar*; a brocade trench; a bralette in lace, studded with Swarovski crystals—that were all so distinctive that even today they remain recognizable as his.

The Tahiliani aesthetic influenced young designers who had worked at the label. With a revolving door of designers moving in and out, each left their own imprint and took with them echoes of their former boss. An open economy brought collaboration with international pattern makers. Notable among them is Belgin Vehbi who did jackets with rounded shoulder pads and toiles, leaving her fingerprints over the 2007 ready-to-wear line. The collection featured

many firsts, from a handloom *kimkhab* trench, a jacket in a banana fibre drape, to a *kediyu*-inspired jacket from Gujarat. In a break from the traditional runway format, most models walked in black in a collection that was severe yet clean. Under the direction of a French stylist, the show highlighted a new modernity at the Wills India Fashion Week. When the ready-to-wear line came to an end, the show was stopped. Tahiliani introduced a new logo and *prêt* line with different fabrics, treatment, silhouettes, and price points. This lasted two seasons and was stopped because the house was unable to manage the numbers, but it was a nod to what Tahiliani loves most—easy-breezy fashion.

—

"In the lobby of Delhi's Grand Hotel, which is hosting the fashion week shows, there are tank tops, crop tops, micro minis, denim corsets, capri pants and embroidered bustiers— but very few saris."
                                                    —*The Guardian*, 2005

Would the sari have new iterations in fast and fine fashion? Could it suffer the same fate as Japan's kimono and China's cheongsam, as exotic attire for festivities in the fast-urbanizing cities? Perhaps India needed "the invention of tradition," an idea coined by Eric Hobsbawm, a Marxist historian. The concept introduced an element of invention in cultural tradition as a way to bridge the gulf of years to keep the past alive.[5] Would it be possible to argue that modernity and tradition are not only inseparable but can be seen as complementary rather than antagonistic forces? Or was the need of the hour an ideological "detraditionalization"[6] where a politicization of tradition was needed to combat traditional norms that are threatened by occurrences such as globalization.

This lamé crinkle sari gown made its debut in 2013 at the amfAR show for AIDS research in Cannes (*above*). Tarun Tahiliani is seen fitting supermodel Karlie Kloss ahead of the show (*facing page*).

There would be a need to seek authenticity to a point in time when culture was uncorrupted by commercial development, but Tahiliani would have to add an invention to ensure it remained contemporary. "Fashion as a Western construct didn't exist in India in the 1980s. The sari has always been there. If I parachuted down then, I would know which part of the country I was in from the way people draped themselves, the textiles they wore. But today, India is becoming generic," says Tahiliani.

Tahiliani thought of the body, the cloth that covers it, and the space created by the union of these elements. He incorporated traditional handicrafts with the latest technologies, visited historic regions, and cultivated age-old techniques of embroidery while adhering to the strictest construction in Western tailoring. His clothes would be of the past and the present, a harmonious meeting of tradition and contemporary life.

—

The Great Recession of 2008 signalled the end of the dream run of the economy. The Big Four Spring Fashion Weeks—New York, London, Milan, and Paris—coincided with the fall financial meltdown and several retailers said sales of expensive fashion, especially clothes, had come to a standstill at the end of September.[7]

Before the 2008 fashion calendar was announced, Tahiliani had been labouring over a big idea that had an integration of East and West at its core. For him, a top could be a Western tunic, a dress, or a *kurti*. "Tarun always taught people different ways to wear the same piece in different settings," recalls Aseem Kapoor. On the night of the show, models strode down the runway with a belt that flashed his idea in red, bearing the words "India Modern". The juxtaposition was highlighted as a model in a leather jacket, reminiscent of an haute biker babe, walking past a Kathak dancer. Devoid of fads and distractions, Tahiliani changed his focus from catering to the international market to catering to India. "I don't want to compete in the dress market. They are not difficult to make, but what is my identity in that?" he asked.

Each collection was meticulously researched and developed while Tahiliani was preoccupied with making the Indian aesthetic more accessible in his ready-to-wear collections. He softened the drama of embroidery by using it sparsely, choosing to look beyond embellishment and towards construction and architecture. In daily design meetings, Tahiliani spoke of updating the look, experimenting with in-built brassieres and Grecian tunic drapes. He spoke of a new idea, to be able to create a structured silhouette out of a sari and, even though there were near-constant attempts to make a draped sari, for a while it seemed out of technical reach. Tahiliani sketched a single piece of cloth

In 2011, Lady Gaga came to India to perform during the Formula 1 Grand Prix. She was sent a selection of clothes to wear for the interview with Shahrukh Khan. She chose to wear this jersey concept sari by Tahiliani, refused to take it off after the interview and wore it to her concert. She even snapped off parts of it to make it her own—she explained that she came to India with a suitcase full of clothes, but when she saw this outfit, her jaw dropped, and she decided to wear it for multiple events.

that could spiral around the body to form a bodice and skirt, he explained his vision to mould without clinging. The task fell upon Kulbhushan Rao, who worked on a body form, fastidiously pinning, draping, and sculpting countless variations in different fabrics, from lace to silk. After weeks of pinching fabric, pushing in pins in endless small, and fluttering and flowing movements, when the first sample was made, there was a sweet irony—the first concept sari was created while working on the construction of a gown. They added billowing drapes to the structured silhouette and when it first debuted, it had the industry and clients hypnotized. Tahiliani made the sari accessible, even if it was made in a more body-conscious style, and it was one of his greater innovations. To be able to zip it up without wrapping the six metres of fabric was a celebration of the craft.

In the collections that followed there was a union of English tailoring with Indian fabrics, where a tweed jacket was made of Indian wool and a sequined jacket had a draped *pallu*. Soon enough, draping, which was primarily a part of couture, became more prominent in ready-to-wear with the introduction of slub jersey and soft viscose. When the peplum draped top dropped, it became a classic Tahiliani look. Equally exciting was his foray into draped dresses, from *chikankari* to *bandhani*, which were the roadmap to India Modern and marked Tahiliani's initial fascination with the sadhu's drape. From then on, Tahiliani made clothes that were so clever that at times it was difficult to figure out how to wear them. Two years after his first attempt at the draped sari, it debuted on stage during Lady Gaga's maiden performance in Delhi's F1 after-party celebration. A year earlier, Lady Gaga, one of the world's biggest popstars, had stunned the world in a meat dress at the 2010 MTV Awards, and when she first appeared in a Tahiliani drape on stage in Delhi in 2011, the press asked: "Is it a sari or isn't it?"

Tahiliani had sketched classical goddess-wear, body fitting yet flattering, and Rao created an ivory ensemble in French chiffon with silk jersey. At a time when female empowerment was being defined as female undressing, Lady Gaga revealed layer after layer on stage until there was nothing left but a high-legged bodysuit with chains. Midway through her performance, she called out to the designer, "I was looking at all my outfits backstage to come out and then I said, well, this sari is much prettier than anything else I brought with me so what I did is I took this sari and ripped it to shreds and made it a little bit New York." Was this then a Western sari?

The link between fashion and modernity was expounded by Friedrich Nietzsche in 1878. For him, fashion was a break from the national costume and a positive force driving modernity. India's tryst with fashion as a Western construct began during colonial rule, when aristocratic Indians started adopting sartorial elements of their colonial masters since it was fashionable to "talk English and walk English". Textiles were anglicized and there was a change in motifs with the introduction of lotuses and tulips. Of great importance was the role of Jnanadanandini Devi Tagore, Rabindranath Tagore's sister-in-law, who transformed the single sheath worn by Indian women by introducing pleats to it and paired it with a tunic-like *shemij*, an adaptation of the Victorian chemise that eventually became the blouse. With the adoption of the petticoat, a new aesthetic for the sari was born. It was through attire that the lines between the colonizer and the colonized were easier to blur, shifting the boundaries between nativity and modernity.

Tradition is very important to Tahiliani. The fusion of the most basic of materials and ancient of traditions with new and innovative techniques is what has kept his brand at the forefront of fashion—technically, if not always critically—for the past twenty-five years. The question for him is how timeless, and relevant, his clothes are. "We've made the sari funky with a corset and aimed to keep the sari in fashion so

that it can be worn in a modern way. I keep telling brides that you are not playing a role where one day you are this Western thing and the other day you are traditional. You've got to play yourself," he says.

—

By 2013, Tahiliani was in complete control of the India Modern aesthetic. In the Kumbhback Collection, he had pushed draping to its limits and handled texturing with panache. Through the wizardry of perfectly placed seams, ombre effects, and ruffled edges, the aesthetic of the sadhu was reproduced. A draped jersey dress executed by Aseem Kapoor with crushed fringes created texture at its maximum effect. Years of experiments with countless metres of satin and chiffon and conversations with Pooja Haldar resulted in Tahiliani's dhoti-sari, which was at once a *nauvari* and a draped sari from Orissa. It was the sort of outfit that showcased the poetic work of human hands, a piece that could transition from a village to a music festival to Delhi's North Block with equal ease. With Kanika Gupta in accessories, bohemian head pieces mingled with jewel-encrusted clutches completed the look.

From then on, there was everywhere to go: a tweed gilet with a concept sari, a *kanjivaram* drape, a scooping up of the sides of a jersey dress in the style of the *sadhvi*s. A mastery

over cut was married with the infinite number of ways a sari could be worn that outlined the curving lines, contouring the shape of the body. From the Kutch collection to the Tarakanna, it was an illustration of how expressive Tahiliani had become as a designer. His motto had become "Make it layered, make it visual and, most of all, make it personal."

By the time Tahiliani debuted the Singh Twins Collection, countless videos on YouTube attempted to decode Tahiliani's concept saris. It was his nonchalant style of draping, with tops cut so long that they could be worn in different proportions with dhoti pants or without. Crucially, Tahiliani was looking back and the fashion architecture was an ode to Milan. Much like the digital tees of 2003, the collection was constructed from dazzling computer-digitized prints and was hyper-graphic, with colour block silks in drapes. The jewel vest with harem pants was updated to a Singh Twins print on a halter with harem pants. With drapes in ombre, it was kitschy and wild but technique was at the forefront, containing pieces such as a cowl skirt and a lungi with a *gara* in georgette. On that runway, Tahiliani debuted the jumpsuit dhoti-sari, its navy chiselled pleats and folds elongated the silhouette and illustrated the possibilities of a constructed sari.

In the end, India Modern was the modernity of the clothes, the architecture, the timelessness. It was and is an assimilation of the East and West that creates garments that are a celebration of a connected world.

*"Nature, and man,
the field and the
knower of the field,
knowledge and that which
is to be known—all this
O' Kesava,
I desire to learn."*

SRIMAD BHAGAVAD GITA 13:1

"Shortly after I started Ensemble, the textile guru Martand Singh gave me three amazing catalogues: one of the Costumes of Royal India exhibit that had shown at the Metropolitan Museum of Art in New York, the second was of a Japanese catalogue and the third was of a show called Vishwakarma, a documentation of the master craftsmen in India followed by an exhibition. For years, I used the Vishwakarma catalogue as a guidebook and visited all the areas it covered. It was a bible of master craftsmen for me. In Bhuj, I went to see block printers, *ajrak* printers, and small villages where they did the *abhla* (mirror work), and that is how my education in Indian craft began. My colleague, Anuradha Amin, and I drove to every printer, embroiderer and textile person in the farthest corners of Kutch. The mud wall villages and the beauty of their work, tribal yet sensuous, had an everlasting impact on me. Perhaps, I felt at home here because of my Sindhi roots. I had to learn so much more before I could translate their incredible drapes into a structured form."

KUTCH

Spring/Summer 2011

"Twenty-one years after
my first visit to the area, I
came across Rohit Chawla's
photographs of Kutch
and this rekindled my
fascination with the region.
We did a collection based
on my memories and the
feelings they evoked in me.
This collection remains
one of my favourites—our
version of the *kediyu* with
bias flaps, ribbons, bias
cones and churidar sleeves
in *malkha*."
KUTCH SPRING/
SUMMER COLLECTION 2011

"In their sameness, each person we saw in Kutch was fiercely different. It was the opposite of cloning, though in fact they wore almost identical textiles that were draped entirely differently on each body."

TARUN TAHILIANI

MALMAL X KHADI

"I discovered a textile called *malkha*, started by a wonderful revivalist, Uzramma, in Hyderabad. *Malkha* derives its name from a combination of the first three letters of the words *malmal* and khadi. It felt like a cotton *shahtoosh*, for lack of a better description." It is clear to see the inspiration derived from the shepherd's attire (*facing page*) of the dhoti translated as an off-white *malkha kediyu* (*above*) worn over a slip dress, also in *malkha*, that stems from the dhoti form.

Malkha became a staple with sushi voile separates and monochromatic *bandhani*, which is shown in these pieces as a draped corset and a long tunic with an attached *malkha* drape and salwar.

"Into the recesses, on the craft trail."

TARUN TAHILIANI

These are different looks for men and women, based loosely on the *kediyu* and *kafni* pajama that is worn in Kutch—the dhoti as a draped form recurs through the collection, with a little smattering of simple A-line dresses, *kediyu* jackets, and *chikankari*. As a backdrop to the show, Tahiliani used a series of photographs by Rohit Chawla of the people of Kutch.

Two examples of playful and contemporary takes on the traditional clothing of Kutch. Diandra Soares (*above*) wears a turban and black georgette draped kaftan inspired by the billowing cotton dhotis men wear in Kutch, while showstopper Shilpa Shetty (*facing page*) wears a tulle top with mother-of-pearl sequins and shells with a *malmal* and tulle lehenga with *gotta* borders.

Millions gather at the confluence of the Ganga, Yamuna and the mythical Saraswati, a mind-boggling tide of humanity arriving in organized waves to cleanse themselves with a holy dip.

THE MAHAKUMBH 2013

"The year (2013) that I went to the Kumbh Mela was touted to be the largest gathering of humanity at one place. People from around the world had come to observe the rigorous discipline, fantastic control and the incredible spectacle of faith—Harvard University had sent a group to study the spatial, social and logistical elements of the mela. But I was there for another reason.... No place on this planet gets to witness so many people wearing clothes and fabrics draped in so many unique styles in one place. The many sadhus, *rishis*, devotees—both male and female—wear different hues of saffron lungis, dhotis, saris, *bundi* jackets, waistcoats with dreadlocks and strings and strings of *rudraksha malas* in the fiercest, most unique individual expressions but using the simplest cotton fabrics. I went to experience, absorb, and learn. From this trip emerged our Kumbhback Collection of 2013."

KUMBHBACK

Autumn/Winter 2013

"This sadhu's use of rudraksha malas and the way in which he layers them to create an adornment for himself could serve as inspiration to fashion designers world over..... We did our own version, which was less costume and more wearable."

TARUN TAHILIANI

A draped jersey shirt
with a *bandhani* swing
shirt with the specially
crafted organza
fringed scarves and
felted *rudraksha*.
AUTUMN/WINTER 2013

A sadhu at the Kumbh Mela wearing a bright orange dhoti and a mango-*kesar* coloured shawl with a fringe. We took inspiration from his attire to design our own version (*facing page*) that starts with a saffron full skirt and is draped with a pleated hip-yoke and a crushed *chanderi* shawl that is wrapped around and arrives at the hand with an interesting fit. We accessorized the look with a necklace made of shells, beads and feathers—as glamorous as any bejewelled neck piece. This marked one of the first variations of the sari drape."

AUTUMN/WINTER 2013

"This collection is very special to the entire team. The ability to twist and turn simple fabrics into these wonderful interpretations of one of our biggest celebrations was very exciting. Models wore long *chotis* with fabric flowers to look like *genda*s along with cashmere wraps made especially for us in Nepal, which were used to add further layers to the drape. We experimented with using traditionally masculine drapes on women, making it our own India Modern."
AUTUMN/WINTER 2013

"India is much more than colour and surface embellishment—the draped form came long before one had the others. It is a basic instinct."

TARUN TAHILIANI

"Sadhus usually wear unstitched garments in shades of saffron as they symbolize renunciation and show that they have moved beyond the material realm. We used the same principles and applied them to the collection that included organza, cashmere, and simple cotton fabrics to reflect this idea of spirituality." Archana Akil Kumar wears a scarf with jagged edges and a jacket that has multiple layers of organza. AUTUMN/WINTER 2013

"*The Kumhhback Collection marked a new energy—
raw, beyond India's peacocks and palaces. Was
it androgynous—yes and no. It is how we have
dressed ourselves for thousands of years—our
visual, sartorial identity since time immemorial.*"

"There is nothing as exuberant as the Singh Twins when it comes to colours and vibrancy, and the fact that they put perspective into the miniature school of painting is a fantastic evolution. But more than anything else, their work has a uniqueness—a point of view that fought art school pressure to make itself heard!"

TARUN TAHILIANI

Tahiliani discovered the Singh Twins at the National Gallery of Modern Art, Mumbai. They exhibited miniatures that were painted with perspective and straddled two worlds. Each one with its own story—symbolic and metaphorical. These originated from the sisters—Rabindra and Amrit Kaur—who were born and brought up in Liverpool, and whose first big exposure to India was when their father drove them on a bus from Liverpool to Kanyakumari and back... an 11-month excursion that changed the way they looked at art. At art school, when they expressed an interest in miniatures, they were mocked and laughed at for being old fashioned. They dress identically and only in Indian clothing such that you cannot tell one from the other. Their story is as fascinating as the narratives they tell through their work. Tahiliani's new collection was inspired by their colours, motifs and forms. The miniature style of painting translates beautifully to digitally printed clothing.

SINGH TWINS

Spring/Summer 2015

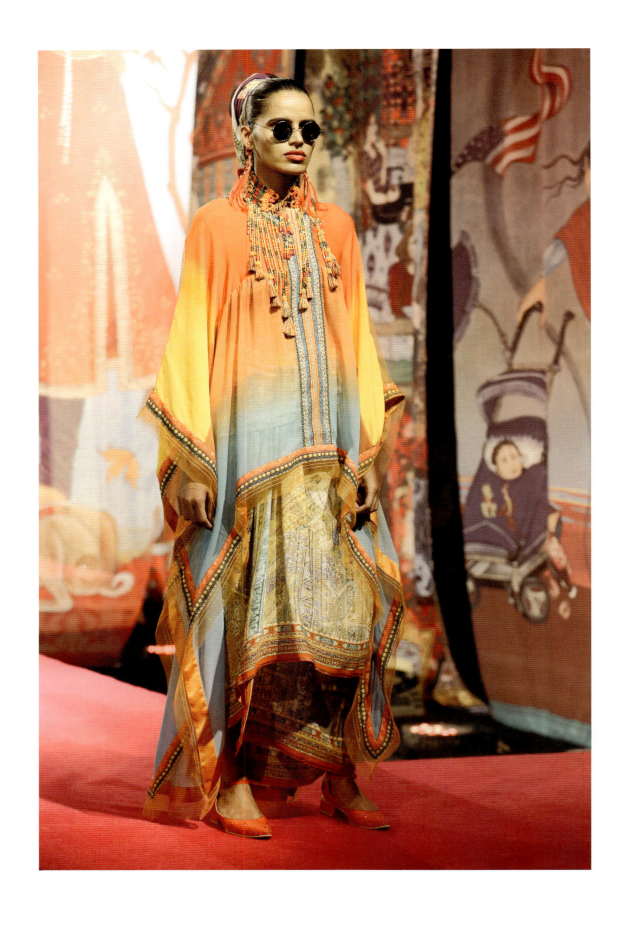

UNION BANCAIRE PRIVEE □

bar birreria pizza

PROFUMERA

Douglas

AERE CIVIVM COND

"Their (Singh Twins) paintings depict the tussle between traditional values and global modernization and the westernization of ideas. We added quilting and our own interpretations of fashion. Some likened it to Versace in the '80s, but with Indian prints, motifs and colours."
SPRING/SUMMER 2015

Amrit and Rabindra with Tarun Tahiliani who dressed them in identical dupattas for the show.

Honey charmeuse in
a sensual drape with
a peplum inspired by
the costumes worn by
Bharatanatyam dancers.

her wedding to businessman Raj Kundra—a burgundy and red sari embellished with Swarovski crystals, it looked traditional yet embodied the comforts of contemporary dressing. "The urban fashion-loving girl today has travelled the world, studied hard, and may even play soccer, yet she wants to look good. Her go-to is the concept sari. I think some of them are never going to put on a normal sari. Now whether that is right or wrong, I do not know... It is what it is."

While it is difficult to put a date to the genesis of the sari as a one-piece garment, as scholars have many different theories, we know it is one of the world's oldest garments, and one of the reasons for its survival is that it has adapted. As Dr. Jay points out, "There are some sari-purists in India who say a sari can't be stitched, and who would even be quite horrified about using pins to secure a sari. But, actually, if you look at the ways women have adapted and countered the challenges presented by wearing a draped piece of cloth, they've always used things like safety pins or a stitched border and fall to help secure the sari and ensure it hangs properly. A pre-draped sari is a logical extension of those everyday dress practices."

For many, the concept sari today serves as an introduction to the drape, and they then experiment with many striking forms of it, which includes the ever-present traditional sari. Author and textile historian Rta Kapur Chishti writes in her book *Sari: Traditions and Beyond*, "Although it is a fast disappearing garment for everyday wear, the sari will survive as special occasion wear." And in many ways, it is the "cocktail" (first made popular by Indian *maharani*s in the 1920s) and now the "concept" version of the sari that has ensured it remains a garment Indian women turn to for special occasions. As did Madhuri Dixit, the renowned Hindi film actor, when the Marrakesh Film Festival bestowed her with a special honour in 2015. Incidentally, it also is my go-to garment. I wore a Tahiliani concept sari for the launch of *Harper's Bazaar* India in New Delhi in 2009 and at many red carpet events now in Dubai. And my love of the drape can be credited to the fact that Tahiliani made his designs seem so easy and flattering to wear.

What has kept the sari alive is that it adapts with time—in many ways, one could call the sari "the first garment of Indian fashion". As Delhi-based writer and curator Mayank Mansingh Kaul says, "The sari as it is worn largely today—with the *pallu* going up the left shoulder of the body—is known to have become a pan-Indian phenomenon only in the 19th century." There are many nuances to the sari, as there are many ways to wear one, and, historically, every state and region of the country has had its own drape styles. "There is no one way to wear a sari," notes Rta Kapur Chishti in her book, and the same goes for its younger, more trend-driven cousin, the concept sari. In the archives of Tarun Tahiliani, you will find many iterations of his favoured drapes—from the saris in metallic tulles and crinkled nets that sat next to pearlesque *chikankari*, embroidered goddess-like drapes in his 2013 Gold Collection to the colourful joyous retro folk-inspired trouser sari worn with a gilet from his Singh Twins Collection in 2015. The latter collection was inspired by the British-Indian artist sisters Amrit and Rabindra Singh, who helped revive miniature painting as an art form.

The trouser-style concept sari of this collection was very much in line with the androgynous ripple having a strong moment across the fashion world at the time and so added a cool factor to the drape. A year earlier, Sonam Kapoor had chosen to wear a black and white chiffon dhoti drape from the Tarun Tahiliani label to a music album launch, and it received much praise from the Indian media. "I think one must always make things more contemporary. Times have changed—women are not just sitting down together at special occasions. There is a lot of movement; they wear heels, are outdoors, and like to dance. Clothes must allow for it all. Our experimentation made the sari become more relevant. It was no longer an intimidating garment that only your grandmother wore and forced you to wear. It became a thing of fashion and was coveted. It became something young fashion girls wanted to wear," explains the designer. His body-con concept sari worn with an obi (belt) is now an iconic part of Indian contemporary fashion's history.

The concept sari is here to stay and is currently de rigeuer in most Indian designer collections. For Tarun Tahiliani, it's the backbone of many of his collection as reflected in his 2020 Spring/Summer capsule collection named "The Drape Series", which is an ode to this silhouette. Incidentally, this collection came out in the year that marked his 25th year in the business, making it one of special significance. By adding a tailored touch, he had turned a draped length of cloth into a constructed garment. The sari that you now see on the ramp, on the red carpet, and in fashion campaigns is rarely unstitched. Like all good fashion, the arrival and popularity of this style gives us a strong insight into the changing attitudes of women. As Dr. Jay says, "A pre-draped sari is a logical extension of those everyday dress practices.... The term 'concept sari' has been around for a few years now, but I've noticed it being used more often recently. Maybe that's part of how Indian fashion is gradually developing its own language for innovation." As

"We coined the term 'concept sari'. It was when I sold an embroidered petticoat—still commonly worn with a long dupatta by young women in the South. Once you attach this dupatta to the base, you can style it in different ways."

TARUN TAHILIANI

demonstrated by supermodel Winnie Harlow who wore a floral Tarun Tahiliani sari with a fluted bikini corset-style blouse on the cover of *Vogue* India's March 2020 edition, the drape—now known as "the Winnie Harlow sari"—looked like it was the perfect ensemble to lounge in while on a beach-island escape.

With his concept sari, Tahiliani has given women a design that has the power to transform them into a modern-day maharani. This is something that Gen Z has become aware of too. When Shanaya Kapoor chose a lilac hand-embroidered concept sari, social media applauded the look. Today, when one documents the history of Indian fashion, Tahiliani's concept sari fatures as an integral part of that story. The first ever international museum show that celebrates the sari was held in 2023 at London's Design Museum. Entitled "The Offbeat Sari" it examines how the sari has evolved to become an integral part of contemporary dressing in recent years. The 2010 couture sari worn by Lady Gaga has been selected to be a part of this show. There is no question that the way Tahiliani has integrated the beauty of this age-old but still living dress form, the regal elegance of its drape with the ease of contemporary tailoring, will perhaps be his abiding legacy to contemporary Indian fashion.

The most dapper of
them all, actor Rahul
Khanna seen in a custom
chocolate velvet appliqué
cropped sherwani with
cotton velvet jodhpurs.
AUTUMN/WINTER 2015

08

THE NEW MAN

THE NEW INDIAN MAN
FINDS HIMSELF

An uneven road zigzags down Vasant Kunj to Tahiliani's home, a secluded farmhouse. Tucked away behind emperor palm and silver oak trees is his sanctuary, filled with a sprawling collection of art and objets d'art. These read like a chronicle of his journey, in objects. Spaces are imbued not simply with good taste but with a point of view, and a large photograph amidst a collection of ostrich eggs speaks volumes.

It is a moody portrait by Rohit Chawla of a man from Gujarat's nomadic Rabari tribe. His cotton white *kediyu angrakha* is untied, revealing a giddy polyester printed T-shirt in a commingling of traditional and modern aesthetics. His dhoti, wrapped in layers, is secured with a belt, and a large turban on his head signifies seniority in the tribe. For Tahiliani, the image encapsulates an almost perfect representation of menswear in a country abounding in complexities of identity. The image is devoid of clichés associated with rural and modernizing India; it is one where polyester sits with the softest cotton, where a garment is worn again and again, where past and present seamlessly coexist.

It is this vision that encapsulates the essence of Tahiliani's vision for menswear: traceability, cultural identity, spirituality, and sustainability.

—

It was the summer of 1991 and Tahiliani had settled into his first atelier at Villar Ville, an elegant early-Edwardian building across the road from the Gateway of India in Bombay. Coiffed women and coy brides were the first to come through the wooden doorway, and, on their heels, following the gentle breeze from the Arabian sea, came a new client: the groom.

Reluctant customers, unaccustomed to rolls of fabric, patterns, and pins, men were dressed in embroidered paisley kurtas on a bed of sharp sherwanis. With an eye for detail, Tahiliani approved every swatch of fabric, sourced the finest Benarasi silk for the turbans, and paired them with embroidered shawls. Famed clients were surprised to discover the designer pinning achkans and *bundi*s himself. Despite the regular orders that accompanied bridal commissions, menswear remained a small operation, with a few tailors bent over the pattern table, sewing and cutting, while Tahiliani sketched sherwanis, jodhpurs and *peshawari*s. Watching over every stitch, he introduced trellising and pintucking and added textures—from *resham* to French knots—in an attempt to establish new techniques for men.

The year 1991 proved to be a seminal one for independent India as prime minister P.V. Narasimha Rao and his finance minister Manmohan Singh presented the Parliament with a new economic policy that undid the restrictive rules of

A sharply manipulated black jersey and crêpe jacket with a one-of-a-kind Viren Bhagat-designed buckle on an embroidered belt to complete the look.
AUTUMN/WINTER 2013

"Licence Raj". When civil aviation was opened to private operators in 1992, Tahiliani designed the uniforms for Jet Airways employees, putting the men at the check-in counters and stewards on board the aircraft in classic midnight-blue suits with a single lapel. The following year, he dressed the staff at the Oberoi Hotel—designing several mood boards with different stories—from the bell boys to the waiters at the restaurant Kandahar.

For Tahiliani, the vision of India lay not in five-star hotels alone but in villages across the country. In 1995, he road-tripped across Kutch in Gujarat, in a white Ambassador and picked up colourful *abhas*, the traditional attire of the Memon, Khatri, and Kojra communities. The fine thread-work and embroidery, from sequins to *baadla*, in different shades of gold lent itself beautifully to the men's collars, which Tahiliani replicated in molten, dull tones for an antique finish. Such subtle discoveries feminized menswear, using fabrics and details traditionally reserved for women. He explored the androgynous abilities of classical outfits and, in doing so, freed a wardrobe long smothered by colonialism and globalization.

—

India has a sartorial tradition dating back thousands of years. It was the first country to cultivate cotton during the Indus Valley civilization; Vedic literature references dyed garments; cave paintings at Ajanta from the 2nd century BCE show men in dhotis while the Chola murals at the Brihadisvara temple depict kings in intricate beaded headpieces as early as the 1st century CE. During the Gupta period, Greek-inspired drapes were common and the arrival of sewn tunics, trousers, and high boots signal Central Asian connections.

The Delhi Sultanate from 1206 to 1526 was characterized by Islamic Afghan and Turkish dynasties that ushered in robes, gowns, and coats in extravagant fabrics. During the Mughal era, alongside the presence of airy cotton and velvety wool, was the courtly coat woven with gold thread. *Malmal*, the fine muslin cloth from Bengal, was sought throughout Asia, Africa, the Middle East, and Europe and dated its popularity to the time of ancient maritime connections. The imperial court patronized local textiles and the Mughal miniatures left an impression on early European missionaries and traders who praised the beautiful attire depicted therein.

This rich legacy was undone under the British Raj.

For its crowning colony, the Empire fashioned its subjects in garments prudent to Victorian style. Men were put in sherwanis and traditional styles were turned into nightwear. The administrators used clothing as a tool to separate caste from class as they created an Indian political elite who were dressed in attire chosen by the rulers. By the 1920s, when the calls for independence grew louder, costume became a political statement.

The styles and textiles of rural India were adopted by leaders of the Indian National Congress in order for them to connect with the masses. Mohandas Karamchand Gandhi, in a dhoti, shawl, and chappals, communicated a message of freedom from the colonial market system. Class-conservative Jawaharlal Nehru and Vallabhbhai Patel, who wore sherwanis, achkans, and churidars, were associated with the courtly and bourgeois urban elite. So crisp was Nehru's image that his achkan with a mandarin collar, morphed into the "Nehru jacket", was worn by the Beatles on stage in 1965 and the *New York Times* noted "excellent activity in the Nehru jacket and the Nehru-collar short-sleeve shirt rack" in New York on April 21, 1968. But the sherwani, perceived as a Mughal garment and a symbol of Indian style, had its origins in British construction and fit.[1]

—

Upon his move to Delhi in 1995, Tahiliani looked towards decolonizing the Indian wardrobe. He sought references from history and studied garments illustrated in the *Akbar Nama* and stylistic variations under different rulers. With a dedicated menswear team, he altered the knee-length coat, making it longer in an adaptation of the style during Shah Jahan's reign and tapered the waist like they did in the 18th century. He refined the constructions of the achkan, *bandhgala*, and sherwani by working on the armhole and fitting the bust, adding darts and side seams. He sourced shoulder pads that gave the garments a stronger line, loosened the *bandhgala* collar, and sought an alternative to the *nada* by adding an elasticated back with a zipper. Cummerbunds accentuated the waist and flattened the stomach and came with a velcro patch for an easier wear while pre-pleated shawls were clipped to the shoulder for security. Crucially, Tahiliani added a lining with each piece in the softest cotton, like the Mughals did, to keep the men cool.

"Men, especially, don't want to suffer in the name of beauty," says Tahiliani.

At the second installation of the Lakmè India Fashion Week in 2001, Tahiliani returned to Bombay for a homecoming at the Taj Mahal Hotel. Deep in last-minute fittings, Tahiliani had an idea to play with the tropes of the fashion show and opened with a six-foot puppet. He named her Basanti,

In Tahiliani's experiments with *bandhgalas*, the open V with layered pockets was an instant hit. A fine wool crêpe *bandhgala* with gunmetal *zardozi* is worn here over a pleated front kurta. Cropping the length of the *bandhgala* modernizes the look.
AUTUMN/WINTER 2013

inspired by Hema Malini's character in *Sholay*. She was a caricature of a woman, with swollen lips, a huge bosom, and an exaggerated body, and 'leapt' around the ramp, scandalizing the front row, the newly-formed fashion press, and buyers. "It was a different world then," recalls Sumeet Nair, Executive Director of the FDCI, who remembers when shows were longer, unlike the militaristic rigour of today.

Then came the clothes, a pure menswear collection from the maestro of women's couture. Models walked to the sound of Madonna reciting Rumi and the collection displayed a strict adherence to traditional suiting techniques spliced with *chikan* and slimming cuts in bold fabrics. It was an original debut with male models in linen and ankle-length trousers draped in sarongs inspired by Tahiliani's trip to Bali and the casual chic of the bohemian set. When a model walked out in a *chikan* shirt, the collection pushed the boundaries of what menswear could look like, proving that it is possible to be surprised by fashion, in the best way. The garments caught the eye of the pioneering Japanese retailer Choichiro Motoyama's son Kuchiro, who picked up the menswear pieces for his flagship store Sun Motoyama in Ginza, to be sold in the womenswear department.

—

In the wake of Independence, as a new India took shape, a great fashion divide appeared from one generation to the next as the pant-shirt replaced the kurta-dhoti and lungi. Crucial in this transformation were four British scientists and innovators—John Whinfield, James Tennant Dickson, W.K. Birtwhistle, and C.G. Ritchie—who created terylene, the first synthetic fabric, in 1941. Terylene was durable and cheap but uncomfortable. As scientists tweaked it further, they transformed the coarseness into a silkiness and named it polyester. In India, polyester's popularity was in part due to the woes of the country's partition that occurred along with Independence. After Partition, the textile industry in India had come to a standstill as the major cotton-producing regions were now in Pakistan while the mills were in Bombay. Sensing an opportunity, a young businessman called Dhirubhai Ambani entered the sagging textile industry in 1966 and set up Reliance Textiles with two circular and two warp-knitting machines and rose to become the chief player in the Bombay yarn market.

In a changing economy characterized by speed, efficiency, and convenience, polyester became the fabric of choice— the "French fries and Coke" of the textile industry. Rows of tailors dotted Indian cities and Tahiliani recalls wearing polyester paisley shirts as a young boy while most men wore the polyester safari suits or spin-offs of Saville Row suits for less than 500 rupees. It was on the back of every self-respecting Indian businessman or civil servant. In a

1997 essay, the late H.Y. Sharada Prasad, a media adviser to three former Indian prime ministers, commented on the election of I.K. Gujral as prime minister: "Thank God, we have a modern, safari-wearing prime minister at last, and the era of khadi has ended." The disappearance of the dhoti and the lungi signified a deeper structure of desire and would signal India's complete integration into the circuits of global capital.[2] Under the currents of globalization, cosmopolitan identities began replacing identities rooted in culture or nation.

—

In 2003, the benefits of global integration come to fruition. Coupled with sound macroeconomic policy management and the demographic dividend, India's growth rate climbed from 5.5 per cent to 8.9 per cent.[3] Textile and clothing played a crucial role in the economic transformation as the second largest sector, employing 35 million people contributing 4 per cent to the GDP, and accounting for 3 per cent of world textile exports.[4] During this period of optimism, Tahiliani spotted talent in Aseem Kapoor, a NIFT student who had graduated with the best menswear award from NIFT Bombay.

At the Gurgaon studio, the duo worked towards refining the cut and introduced a host of corrective measures, to the armhole, plackets, and collars, for better construction. They modernized techniques by changing the fusing, and the kurta underwent a small but crucial transformation through the introduction of a cuff. The achkan was updated by shedding the bulk upfront and incorporating a centre back dart for a slimmer cut. The studio introduced the practice of making toiles for menswear in muslin and masters worked fastidiously, folding, nudging, and pleating for better proportion. Tahiliani played with the width and length in his sketches and laboured over buttonholes. In the new swatches that landed on his table, there were fabrics, appliqué, and top-stitch options.

At the Garden of Five Senses show in 2005, Tahiliani introduced a ready-to-wear menswear line that included raw-linen jackets and gabardines, jodhpur trousers with multiple buckles and West-inspired silhouettes in an ivory and beige palette. In their search for materials, Tahiliani and Kapoor visited China in 2008 and discovered a crêpe wool that had stretch and a great fall, and it became a mainstay of the house.

In subsequent collections, the team handled couture and ready-to-wear with equal ease, showcasing swooping asymmetric hemlines punctuated by wide, deliberately languid ruffles while Tahiliani perfected his signature style: a soft take on construction.

The dhoti is quintessential and
one of the oldest Indian drapes.
AUTUMN/WINTER 2014

It was the first Friday in September 2011 and society darlings and magazine editors, bloggers and buyers waited for the doors to open at Tahiliani's Autumn/Winter offering for the Van Heusen Men's Week. Inside the dimly-lit ballroom at the Grand Hotel in New Delhi, a flurry of activity unfolded.

Samandar Manganiar and his troupe of Sufi *qawwals* took their place on the catwalk and a group of volunteers from fashion schools placed the press note, which read "modern *fakirs*/world travellers", on the seats. Holy men in drapes who rejected worldly goods for divinity, *fakirs* were often found at shrines in India, extolling saints in spiritual ecstasy. The term gained popularity during the Mughal era but was also used in the waning days of the British Empire when Winston Churchill called Mahatma Gandhi a "seditious fakir". So, it was a stroke of genius when, seconds after the door opened and the room turned dark, black and white grainy footage from the days of the freedom struggle was projected on the wall.

The show opened to the melody of the *tabla* and *dholak*, as the Sufi *qawwals* sang over the sound of the harmonium. With the first model on the ramp, Tahiliani pushed at the barriers of fashion and showed an open vision of society, showcasing the *fakir* in a space once dominated by royals. Models walked in elegant drapes on a deconstructed silhouette; *malkha* drop-crotch pants; a textured *bandhgala* with scrunched up sleeves; viscose jersey and black and white silk *bandhani* was paired with Italian fabrics; tweed separates with crêpe wool accompanied Rajasthani *juttis*. On one model in a black crêpe wool kurta, a drape ran from the sleeve to the collar, resulting in a deep pleat that was paired with a khaki mandarin-collared shirt and a narrow trouser. The palette mimicked the patina of the colours of dust, from beige to muddy taupe.

—

Tahiliani's journey came full circle during a collaboration with Whitcomb and Shaftesbury, tailors from Saville Row, in 2014. The collection brought together the elements of English fine tailoring in Saville Row's rigid shoulder, high armhole, and defined waist and the joys of a Tahiliani drape. In one piece, Tahiliani united a classic jacket with a *kanjivaram* draped dhoti in ivory on gold. It was a complex creation: the front was a lungi inspired from Punjab and the back was a dhoti, constructed so that it could be pulled on like a trouser. It was paired with a fine quilted *bundi* in rose gold with *zardozi* embroidery and a zero-point collar, a surplice, and a stole. The look—a drape with a Saville Row jacket—was an amalgamation of the East and West, and the combination of a dhoti and lungi was a nod to the north and south of India.

In piece after piece that left the observer guessing whether it was "this" or "that", Tahiliani dared to challenge a long-established premise of modern fashion: its obsession with what comes next. Tahiliani's work allows the wearer to showcase a fantasy of yesterday, today. As the onslaught of globalization continues, the inter-connected flow of goods, ideas, and culture transverses borders. When the digital society that birthed an Instagram ideal speeds the drive of fast fashion, homogenizing the diversity of India, style, which is an expression of identity, is diluted. This economy thrives on inexpensive manufacturing and mass production. As Dana Thomas writes in *Fashionopolis: The Price of Fashion and the Future of Clothes*, "...of the more than 100 billion items of clothing produced each year, 20 per cent goes unsold—the detritus of 'economies of scale'. Leftovers are usually buried, shredded or incinerated."

Tahiliani aspires to the opposite, to the kind of creations that can be worn today and tomorrow and be a part of your wardrobe forever.

Silk velvet cross-over
draped waistcoat with
a linen cuffed kurta
and a dhoti.
AUTUMN/WINTER 2014

"IDENTITY, SPIRITUALITY & SUSTAINABILITY— THE ESSENCE OF THE VISION FOR MENSWEAR."

TARUN TAHILIANI

A royal blue *bandhgala* with gilt embroidery and a fused cummerbund paired with classic black jodhpurs. AUTUMN/WINTER 2013

FACING PAGE: An entire Kanjivaram sari was fashioned into a softly draped dhoti for this look. The *pallu* was cut into the front panels of the waistcoat. AUTUMN/WINTER 2013

The addition of a Tahiliani favourite, the *jamawar* shawl, instantly uplifts a classic sherwani in muted tones, adding courtly charm to the look.
AUTUMN/WINTER 2014

FACING PAGE: A subtle ivory sherwani with graded French knots embellished with pearls and crystals—a crowd favourite.
AUTUMN/WINTER 2014

FACING PAGE: A silk velvet *bandhgala* worn with tapered trousers is an effortless attire designed for any salon in the world.

An example of Tahiliani's experiment with drape even in menswear—a six-button kurta that moves slightly on the bias and cascades onto the right, worn with a churidar and embroidered *juttis*.
AUTUMN/WINTER 2017

Beyond the clichéd ideas of androgyny, Tahiliani's menswear pieces include subtle details like floral embroidery done in the Parsi *gara* style.
AUTUMN/WINTER 2017

Mohair sleeveless
sherwani with silver
buttons and pleated
collars in charmeuse
satin paired with a
dupion silk kurta and a
Kanjivaram dhoti with
satin edging. The dhoti
was crafted out of an
entire Kanjivaram sari in
masculine grey stripes.
AUTUMN/WINTER 2015

The drape tradition was deeply rooted in Indian dressing—turbans, safas, dhotis, lungis, shawls and chaddars were prevalent, but started to vanish as men began to join the work force in colonial India and adopt Western dresses, preferred for their connotations of exposure, progress and wealth.

Examples of Tahiliani tailoring and layering—short kurta worn with a *bundi* teamed with a pair of wedged hem and narrow pants.

FACING PAGE: Bold variations of the classic *bundi*.
AUTUMN/WINTER 2019

"While growing up, I would see the dabbawalas in Bombay wear dhotis and short kurtas and I associated the attire with an old and archaic India. Today, I have a very different point of view. Having rediscovered our Indian identity, I find the modern version of the dhoti with short shirts and a jewel belt incredibly cool and contemporary."

TARUN TAHILIANI

INSET: Rai Pannalal Mehta (Dewan of Udaipur) by Raja Ravi Varma, 1901.

Raja Ravi Varma paintings were the inspiration for many of the structured drapes found in Tahiliani designs—for instance, pre-draped cummerbunds.

Sherwanis, kurtas and *chogas* featuring *zardozi*, *chikankari* and hand-woven textiles—a small design gamut from the house; and a rare appearance by Tahiliani's youngest son, Jahan (*centre*). COUTURE, 2010

The *pagdi*, headgear worn by men, varied in form and stance based on stature. Each region had its own style and textiles which were often embellished with jewels.

FACING PAGE: In a classic crème palette, a pearl encrusted brocade sherwani jacket with *ambi* motifs, over a long, crinkled kurta paints a stately picture.
AUTUMN/WINTER 2012

A blue velvet *bundi*
with fine *zardozi* work
contrasts the stark
minimalism of a
white-on-white
chikankari kurta.
COUTURE 2016

From his early
modelling days, actor
Sidharth Malhotra
in a double placket
chikankari kurta paired
with a *jamawar* shawl.
AUTUMN/WINTER 2016

FACING PAGE: Despite
its various technicolour
iterations, the beauty
of the finest *chikan*
embroidery is best
showcased on muslin.
AUTUMN/WINTER 2016

INSET: Thakur Raja Bakhtawar Singh painted by Fateh Muhammad, 1880, possibly Bikaner. The royal costumes of Rajasthan include a sash tied around the waist known as a *patka*.

FACING PAGE AND RIGHT: Embroidered sherwani paired with embellished cummerbunds inspired by the *patka*s of Rajasthan. AUTUMN/WINTER 2015

"I embroider sherwanis
for men that have a
much lower neckline to
allow ease of movement."
AUTUMN/WINTER 2018

Kutch, the nomads, *malkha*, the colour of sand and subtle block printing on khadi—simpler drapes, trousers that approximate salwars and asymmetry made up the menswear look in 2013.

"MEN, ESPECIALLY, DON'T WANT TO SUFFER IN THE NAME OF BEAUTY."

TARUN TAHILIANI

ABOVE AND FACING
PAGE: An understated
take on quilting—the
chicest way of staying
warm on a cold day.
AUTUMN/WINTER 2017

TT

09

THE STRUCTURED DRAPE

NONITA KALRA

Former Editor-in-chief, ELLE India &
Editor, Harper's Bazaar India

When Tarun Tahiliani and I met earlier this year, it was one of those rare, pleasant mornings where Delhi had pulled out clear, blue skies. We had fixed to be at the Mehrauli store at 9 am and he was already waiting for me as I drove in. The designer has always been a creature of contradiction. On one hand, he is the person you can drink whisky with till 4 am, and on the other, he will be the first person at the factory. Work and play go hand in hand for him. Of late, conversation had been circling around reinvention but that has always been a common theme in his journey as a couturier. Tahiliani is always thinking—about the brand, about what women want, about the future. He was one of the first people I met when I became the editor of a fashion magazine. We became friends over time. Strangely enough, we grew close when I criticized a collection of his. Perhaps that's when we knew we could trust each other. What then followed was a peculiar combination of mad lunches and wild dinners. The adjectives one would use to describe a relationship with Tahiliani are never regular. But they are always real and respectful. There is no other man I can learn from, no other designer who is so thoughtful, so erudite. He is equal parts intellectual and irreverent. He knows his mind, but he likes to get to know your mind too. A month after we last spoke, the country went into the nation-wide lockdown brought upon by the COVID-19 pandemic. During this time, we talked often about what would come next. Over and over again, he reiterated that Tarun Tahiliani needs to go back to the basics. And he did just that. But funnily enough that has always been his vision, his strategy. This is why the below conversation—about fashion, fearlessness, and his favourite technique of draping—is still so valid.

Do you remember when you developed a fascination for draping? Was it when you went to study in fashion school?

You know, that's actually why I went back to school. I don't even know if you're aware of this. We had started Ensemble, and I had done one or two very basic courses at Fashion Institute of Technology (FIT), New York, so I knew there was something out there. And then, in 1989, the Festival of France came to India and it was a huge spectacle. They brought down Yves St Laurent. There was a show at the Gateway of India. They were meant to choose one Indian designer, one model, and one photographer. So, we all sent sketches, and in the shortlist, quite ironically, were Rohit Bal, Suneet Varma, Shahab Durazi, and Tarun Tahiliani, among others. And then, we were whittled down to 20 names and asked to send garments. But there was so much politics that the French just dropped the designer category and decided to take two models instead—Sheena Singh and Marielou Phillips. That really depressed me, as there was an apprenticeship on offer. I said to Sal, "Some Indian should have been good enough to go." And she said, "If you really want to, then go study. Why are you sitting here and whining?" And that's how I went to FIT for their Fashion Design programme.

At that time, when I drew something that approximated a drape, the tailors would gather fabric, like those little curtains at the cinema, and they would think that was draping. Subconsciously, we knew how to drape on a body, but we could not structure it.

Why is draping so integral to India?

I think we got away with it because firstly, there was a lot more draping and muslin in very warm climates because you didn't really need to layer past a point. I think embroidery came with Islam. It's not something that belonged to Hinduism because I don't know of any indigenous embroideries that we did. We wove fabrics. And when I say we, I mean Hindus. I think that the draping itself is something that stayed certainly in a country that has the sari and the dhoti, that's the basis of everything. Unlike the Greeks and the Romans, who basically had the toga and the Doric chiton, our tribal communities have so many different iterations of the drape. There are hundreds of thousands of turbans, saris, and dhotis. Many different ways of wearing a sari from the *nauvari* to the Bengali style. Till we learned some tailoring from the British—the Mughals only brought in the basic *jama*—there was only draping. Part of Indian sensuality was also the layering and transparency. If you look at the miniature paintings and the women, you can see through the cholis. The finer the fabric, the more beautifully it is draped.

How is draping in India different from the techniques used in the West?

In the West, there were two very basic kinds of draping. One was a very tailored look, in wool. So, if you looked at everything that Mr. Dior or Mr. Balenciaga did, it was very precise. There's no fabric here unless you quilt it, even then it doesn't have the same form. And it lacks the malleability of wool. And then there was your Madame Grès sort of thing where she ruched and fluted in silk jersey, or what Norma Kamali did with parachute material. And then came Donna Karan and Giorgio di Sant' Angelo, who died in the early 1990s but had done some wonderful stuff. (Gianni) Versace was incredible too, especially his Australian Wool Collection in 1988. The show ended with Indian model Kirat Young walking down the ramp, and she had that particular amazing lilt. So many designers did different things with drape but they relied entirely on structure. There was no concept of what we were trying to do, which was to semi-drape on the body. We were trying to replicate, not lose, India.

Since drape is such a big part of Indian tradition, was it a common conversation in the fashion fraternity? Or did you have to find your own inspiration?

I think, as you know, most designers don't have a lot of conversations, except post midnight, and those are kind of incoherent. So, I don't think there was a lot of serious conversation around this, but since everyone was visual it would lead you to the next idea because these things are evolutionary. I won't say that I woke up one fine day and had twenty epiphanies. You're always feeding off popular culture. Unlike in the Western hemisphere where everything has been documented for centuries because of portraiture and painting, there are no records in India; nothing till Raja Ravi Varma came along, anyway. So, I had to find inspiration in real life. If you look at photographs of tribal India, and you look at the sadhus—no two are ever alike. That is the genius of India. I've gone on *parikrama*s around Tiruvannamalai, tripping on the music. I have ridden a chariot in the Kumbh. It was wild and hysterical. Everybody is fantastical, from the way they did their hair to the flowers they used. It was unbelievable.

How did you bring this drape home, to the brand Tarun Tahiliani?

This is a hysterical story, which came up when Alia [Allana] interviewed Ajju master [Arjun Godiya]. At that time, Ajju used to work for Bapa Dhragendra, a lovely old man who ran a small business with his sister-in-law. They worked from their apartment and Ajju, one of their young masters, would come on the train from Kalyan and make these little blouses in chiffon with ruffles. I had bought this beautiful *paithani* for Rs. 4,000—a fortune at the time. I wanted it draped a particular way but since we didn't have dress forms, Ajju took it home, stripped down to his underwear, stood in front of the mirror and then figured out how to do it. That's how the first drape sari happened: on a man, because he couldn't get a woman to take off her shirt.

Many years later, when we moved to Delhi (and I had persuaded him to move with us), he used to fit corsets on his wife. I told him if you fit it on her, it is never going to work on anybody else because she was a good Sindhi buxom thing. Actually, Ajju went on the draping journey with me. I sent him to NIFT to do a short course as well. And then Minal Modi would show him Agent Provocateur corsets and explain their construction. You learn from your customers, and, certainly someone like that, who was a friend and became a studio muse.

If you were to define your career in drape, what would be the most seminal pieces that you worked on?

I like what I do now as we get more pared down and, in a way, more modern. Like our *anarkali* with the simple drape, which allows the neck to come really low. It is slightly ruched so it looks crinkled, and a very sheer back allows us to put big pieces of embroidery or just a jewel. The dhoti-sari, the concept sari, I think for me, are special because we have so many iterations—whether they are made in jersey, worn with corsets or just jackets. We have started doing Ikat dhoti drape pants, which can be worn with a little gilet or a bra inside. Everything is used up in the sari; in fact, the *pallu* becomes the gilet. It is like we used to work in the beginning but it works. I'm Indian. I don't aspire to be minimal at all. I like miniatures, I love the layering. I love the pattern. I like that fullness.

Are you both a designer and a stylist?

Always. My sketches have everything down to the last detail. This particular Saturday (in February 2020), I was in Dubai and I had two hours to spare. I spent it buying shoes for my next shoot. I like doing that. I like enduring style. I like that Indian style is enduring. I like the fact that you look the same 20 years later. All the women I found stylish, from Maharani Gayatri Devi to Minal Modi, have changed their fashion a bit with age but their style was always their own, and didn't need to change.

When you started out, did you have some sense of what you were going to do? Where you were going to be?

It is 30 years since Ensemble, and 25 years since Tarun Tahiliani. Before that, it was a little part-time thing, called Ahilian, you know—Tahiliani without the T and the I. I didn't think about it. I don't think. Ever since my sister and I separated the companies, I got this business like a baby on my lap, and now I'm being forced to think. I don't think I've thought a lot before, except about having fun. Enjoying the ride.

Is that what defines your brand—the fact that you really felt your way through it?

Yes. If I felt like doing jewelled T-shirts, I did it. Some things were a commercial disaster. It totally bombed but I had a blast. A lot of things I've done were ahead of their time. Also, I think I left it to those who did the merchandizing too much. They didn't understand what to do with it. We would do the big show, and we'd be on to the next thing the next day. Unfortunately, here you have to see it through to the end because if you don't, it's not transmuted. Too much gets lost in translation, especially with drape and fluidity.

Do you reflect or do you look forward?

I mostly look forward. I only used to think about the short term. But now that I have the business to think about, it's different. You know, by the time you are 57 years old, you will have to start being aware of your waist and your mortality—these two things come at once.

Waste or waist?

When I look back, I think I wasted a lot of opportunities because I jumped around like a child. When we went to Milan, we did a lot of work, we sold in all the top stores, but when I came back again, it just fizzled out. I think, those kinds of investments are great if you follow through with them. Unfortunately, I think, we approached it like excited children because it was too fast, too new. We didn't have precedents, we didn't have anybody to look up to, we hadn't trained with anybody, and so we jumped from one thing to another. For years, I felt very inadequate because I didn't know how to fit. Even as a designer, it takes 10–15 years for your hand to set. You know you can start walking, all infants start to walk, but you don't know until you are 12 if you're going to be a runner or not.... Remember, I started life selling oil-field equipment. For two years, I was almost dead and was only saved by acting in Pearl Padamsee's plays. Sal said I was a terrible actor and should really not have been doing this. But anyway, I had fun and laughed with creative people. When I started the business, Pearl told me, "You will come right back like a church mouse."

You don't think this fearlessness that led to some sort of insanity, is the reason you are successful? Precedent kills any creativity, right?

I've had many adventures because of this fearlessness. I wouldn't trade that for anything. I've travelled around this country with no purpose except to fulfil my visual sense. So, I think, from that point of view, the fearlessness was there because we were at a time where we could afford to

"For me it's just the way people look when they're draped. So even if it's plain black coarse cotton, or muslin, everybody was draping in India because there is very little that was structured, it had been this way for centuries. That is what inspires me."

TARUN TAHILIANI

do it. We weren't that ambitious; we were not measuring ourselves against a bottom line. That changes the way you look at things. I think that now, finally, because you've also got thousands of people dependent on you, there's responsibility. So, I think, at some point it has to change. Suppose I look at someone like Brunello Cucinelli who right now is my hot favourite in terms of just the way that town runs, and the way he's changed people's lives, and the quality of his product. Once you put on a sweater of his, you never want to take it off. It's kind of non-fashion because it's so timeless. You will wear it a hundred times. Only quality can be sustainable. You can't be fast and, you know, cheesy and be sustainable, right? So, it all fits together beautifully. So, from that point of view, I think, our job now is to make sure that we take care of the people in the factory, see how they work, and change people's lives.

I love going to work every day. When I walk through that building, unless I've got a finance meeting, I love it. That big room where we work, it's wonderful. I mean I'm blessed in that way, you know, and we keep evolving.

Thirty years later, what inspires you, and do you ever question why?

I question why we are doing what we do. A lot has changed in 30 years. I think that there's so much more exposure and globalization, money—certainly—and travel. For instance, when our parents' friends came to dinner—we were service kids, and my father had friends come over who were 75 years old—they never had much money, they had a slight homogeneity in the way they dressed. But, within that they were very individualistic. And they were very chic because nobody was trying to be what they were not. Media had not bombarded them, which now is where I feel that continuing colonization comes out.

What has always inspired and excited me, which I don't think we grew up enough seeing in urban India, and certainly not in the cantonments, was what I saw when I started to drive around the country because of fashion—to understand our crafts and textile tradition. I took Mapu's (Martand Singh) book *Vishwakarma* and started driving through Kutch. I would drive for five days and visit every weaver and block printer. I started with trying to learn what they did. But along the way, I started to see a whole lot of other things that, perhaps, as a kid, I was even disdainful of, you know, when we drove around India. I mean, I never looked up. I didn't want rural India. I didn't want anything that was rural India. That was not the world we knew. We were white, we were brown whites, we were trying to be white, and we looked down at Hindi. My whole attitude changed slowly. And I began to rediscover through fashion—which I would never have done otherwise—a whole aesthetic that started to make sense in a context that was not superimposed. It had probably been this way for years. And while I did, of course, like embroideries and things like that, textile for itself has never been my favourite thing. For me, it's just the way people look when they're draped. So even if it's plain black coarse cotton, or muslin, everybody was draping in India because there is very little that was structured, it had been this way for centuries. That is what inspires me. Apart from a bit of franticness that "My God, we're just losing all of this stuff!", I personally love draping and I think it's beautiful and it's an identity like the kimono and obi are Japanese, you know?

Let's talk about the first time you took the sari to New York, then.

We were at this birthday party, which got a bit out of hand—all these older women were dancing on the sofa and they called me and said, "You are a designer, wrap us, we want to tie a sari." I just started pulling down the drapes and using them. One of the guests was Carrie Fisher. And I said to myself, "The sari comes to New York at 3 am."

"Our draping techniques have evolved to work with the dynamics of the body, echoing it as it moves with delicateness, sensuality, strength, and grace."

TARUN TAHILIANI

A STUDY IN DRAPE

THE FLUIDITY OF STRUCTURED DRAPING

TT

A jersey draped dress with a reverse *pallu*, worn with a dipped bolero, onto which jewels have been encrusted on the pocket flaps.
AUTUMN/WINTER 2010

FOLLOWING PAGES (194–95): Images from a show portraying an array of *pashminas*, *kalidar* long and short kurtas, capes, corsets, embroidered belts, sushi voiles, shirts, and salwars.
AUTUMN/WINTER 2014

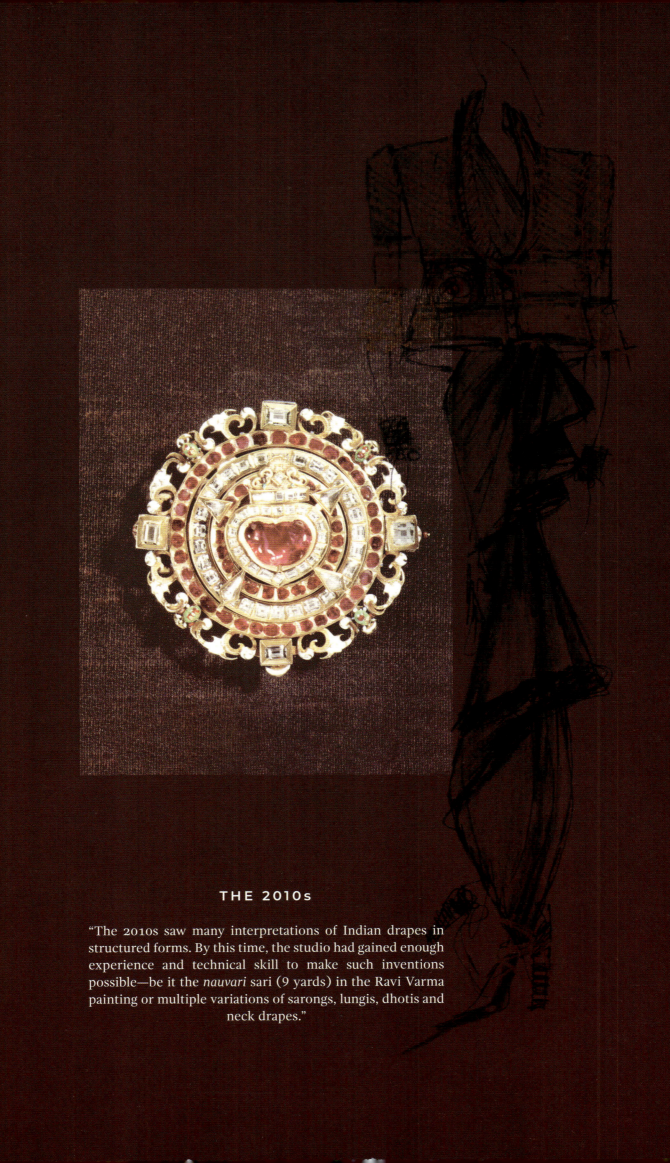

THE 2010s

"The 2010s saw many interpretations of Indian drapes in structured forms. By this time, the studio had gained enough experience and technical skill to make such inventions possible—be it the *nauvari* sari (9 yards) in the Ravi Varma painting or multiple variations of sarongs, lungis, dhotis and neck drapes."

Is it a dhoti? Is it a
lungi? Is it a sari? An
embroidered choli with
a draped concept sari.
AUTUMN/WINTER 2014

FACING PAGE: Lisa Haydon
(*centre*) wears the same
ensemble and on either
side of her are two
variations of the *kalidar*
kurta—one with a narrow
salwar and the other, a
more classic version with
an attached drape.
AUTUMN/WINTER 2014

A satin concept sari references the *nauvari* (9-yard sari) so often depicted in paintings by Raja Ravi Varma (*facing page*). AUTUMN/WINTER 2014

"We are trying to replicate, not lose India."

TARUN TAHILIANI

LIGHTNESS & SHEER

"Textiles used in layering were achieved with finest Indian
fabric made in very sheer counts. Today, I use fine tulle to
achieve a similar effect. It is cool, easy on the eye, ventilates
the body, and is sensual all at once."

Sarong skirt with a drape inspired by the lungi worn
with different bodice variations—from the jewelled
T-shirt to an asymmetrical top with *gara* embroidery
to a waistcoat and a fitted bodysuit worn with a corset.
AUTUMN/WINTER 2015

THE DRIP TECHNIQUE

"In 1989, during a show organized by Bina Kilachand called 'Art Wear Show', I had the good fortune to work with Akbar Padamsee, the great artist who painted, in his own words, 'like the opposite of an excavation'. He used his palette knife to creat layers of paint as is evident in this now famous metascapes. While playing with this technique, I started to drip turpentine and linseed oil through the paint and let it eat the paint away. This is the basis of the painting (*facing page, bottom right*), which was translated into a carpet with ikat borders for the OBEETEE Collection (*facing page, top left*) and the red painting (*facing page, bottom left*) became part of a print in one of our collections."

"Mrinalini Mukherjee, who was one of the fiercest sculptors in India, worked with hemp fibre, ceramics, and cast bronze. She was hospitalized a day before the opening of a major retrospective of her work, 'Transfigurations: The Sculpture of Mrinalini Mukherjee' at the National Gallery of Modern Art, New Delhi, and passed away a few days later in 2015. Her use of draped, coiled and twisted hemp was incredible for layering and it inspired me to dedicate a collection honouring her."

Adi Pushp II, Mrinalini
Mukherjee. Dyed hemp,
1998/99.

FACING PAGE: The
Autumn/Winter 2016
collection inspired by
Mrinalini Mukherjee's
final retrospective.

A spring easy breeze,
where the drape is
an ankle-length dress
worn with a churidar
and the ubiquitous
concept sari, which
is light and sheer.
SPRING/SUMMER
2017

Schiffli, silk georgette and cording paired with a Benarasi cutwork for this textural collection. SPRING/SUMMER 2017

FACING PAGE: *Chikankari* on silk georgette—enhanced by one silk thread and a hand-embroidered motif—in the contemporary drape series. AUTUMN/WINTER 2017

COLOURS OF TT

"I have always loved the colours of sand, ivory, beige, ecru, and taupe, all dip-shaded in Indian *mitti*. The patina of Indian dust has inspired the palette for my spring summer collections year after year."

From left to right: *Chikankari* on printed bases with long asymmetric motifs—referencing the flapper style. A textured satin tape and fringe skirt and pre-draped *anarkalis*. AUTUMN/WINTER 2017

The Tarakanna Collection juxtaposed stardust, constellations, astronomy charts, and star clusters with Mughal-inspired floral and jewel motifs. It renders the essence of the galaxy in striking ombrès and fine embellishments. Lightweight fabrics such as sheer silk, *chanderi*, cotton, georgette, crêpe, *resham*, and the finest Italian tulle move with ease, while tiny Swarovski crystals wink at you. SPRING/SUMMER 2018

INSPIRED BY EGYPT

"I was invited to speak on the history of drape in India at the Indian ambassador's residence in Cairo in March 2018. I felt this was a good opportunity to take our entire design team to Egypt. We started with a visit to the National Museum of Egyptian Civilization in Cairo, travelled up the Nile from Luxor to Aswan and visited the spectacular Tunis, the Valley of Kings and charming villages, docking at the Al Adabiyah port along the way. Having loved Egyptian faience and the fine draping seen in indigenous paintings, the design team was naturally inspired to create a spectacular collection based on what they admired and absorbed during this trip."

Off the plane from Egypt and thinking pharoahs and Tutankhamun. Black and gold, and an asymmetric drape reinvented as a contemporary jumpsuit. SPRING/SUMMER 2019

Draped dresses that
are inspired by saris,
dhotis and lungis and
shot at the Qutub Minar
at sunrise.
SPRING/SUMMER 2020

A playful and elegant
version of the concept
sari in lamé jerseys
paired with sculpted
boned corset bodices
dripping with bits of lace
and crystal.
SPRING/SUMMER 2021

CORSETRY

"Minal Modi and Isabella Blow started the studio on its corsetry journey. Minal loved corsets worn with saris in plain chiffon, and Isabella used them as a base with the clothes she wore and subsequently taught us, having discovered McQueen and other great stalwarts. It started with a sari choli, moved to bodice wear for concept saris, and is now used for as longer blouses worn with lehengas... women love to be held and shaped."

A long fluted evening gown in forest greens with hints of emerald. The classic fluting in small bias pieces of chiffon give the illusion of different shades of green wrapping around the body.
25 YEAR COLLECTION 2020

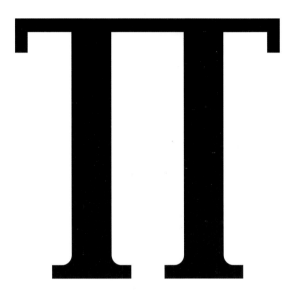

"When I started, I did not realize how powerfully embedded the draped form was. Everyone thinks of India as colour and embroidery or surface embellishment. In fact, it is much more."

TARUN TAHILIANI

11

Gossamer layers of the softest tulle draped around the bride's head create an aura of mystery.
BRIDAL & COUTURE, LATE '90S

BRIDAL & COUTURE

COUTURE IS FANTASY, IT IS A DESIGNER'S LABORATORY

Years before there was a groom, Kajal Chellaram had imagined her wedding day. When she laid her eyes on a pleated kurta in beige cut work by Tarun Tahiliani, she knew she would be a Tahiliani bride. In the summer of 1991, soon after the wedding date was fixed, Chellaram scheduled an appointment. It was Tahiliani's first serious bridal commission. At the meeting in Ensemble, he promised Chellaram a wedding outfit of infinite detail with the finest craftsmanship. The threads of inspiration arose from the temples of India and were rooted in Tahiliani's novelistic attention to detail.

Work began earnestly at Tahiliani's new studio in Villar Ville, opposite the Gateway of India. The team worked on Tahiliani's sketch—a lehenga with a trail and a pleated drape on a belt, reminiscent of medieval England. The smallness of the operation, a studio that was preoccupied with obtaining permission for water supply, lent an intimacy to the enterprise. Those were the dark days of the Bombay riots when waves of communal violence terrorized the city. Despite the uncertainty, Ratna Vyas, the major domo ventured into the embroidery units on Mohammed Ali Road and, for a moment, forgot about the climate of insecurity. She was dazzled by the work of the artisans, hunched over wooden frames, feverishly embroidering silver and gold threads, pearls and beads as they decorated the golden lehenga with *zardozi*. As the big day approached, neighbourhoods were swept by rioting mobs. Embroiders, predominantly from Muslim communities, locked themselves indoors while Tahiliani

and Vyas sat in a darkened studio sewing *butti*s on the veil. On the big day, they chased after the wedding procession with a heavy box in their hands bearing the outfit.

That night, the bride wowed in an attention-grabbing piece but, for Tahiliani, it was also an intriguing study of couture, its possibilities and limitations. The piece weighed more than 12 kilos and imprinted two things upon the designer: weightlessness and craftsmanship. In its traditional form, the wedding lehenga was an outlived vogue. The nature of the dress, though beautiful, inflicted unnecessary hardships. Tahiliani values narrative and context as much as cut or fit and the horror stories of women who lay in bed feverish after their wedding receptions as they struggled under the weight of their garment—most had to wear suspenders to hold it up—did not gel with his worldview of emancipated women. He wanted to strike a balance between the demands of the brides and sensible dressmaking. Like a novelist who divides himself between his characters, one part of Tahiliani sketched late into the night, creating looks that changed the course of fashion while another changed the business of couture.

In 1995, when society darling Jemima Goldsmith wore a Tahiliani gown to worldwide press coverage, the designer's vision was on its way to shaping fashion for a new era. "Back in the day, a lot of brides could not walk but a woman should be free to dance," he said. It was a commitment to liberate women from the *ghunghat* with the introduction of the sheer veil, to ensure they remain full of life and

modern, which saw him dress thousands of brides in a transforming silhouette with a refined sensuality that became the hallmark of Tahiliani's style.

—

Couture is fantasy. It is a designer's laboratory where a commission can inspire collections for years. Couture implies one-of-a-kind pieces of art that push fashion to its very limit. The practice affords the designer freedom, away from commercial restraints, and the pleasure to see the customer walk away with the sensibility of the couturier himself. Genuine couture is not simply about the front or the back of the outfit. It is about what is in between, about the person.

Couture as a business was invented by an Englishman called Charles Frederick Worth in 1858 in Paris. Those were the days of 19th-century splendour where the royal court's social calendar demanded clothes that possessed a certain level of grandeur and pomp, which could only be satisfied with yards upon yards of finery and crinoline gowns to be worn for balls. In the 20th century, Parisian couture underwent a radical transformation at the hands of Christian Dior when he showed his first haute couture collection on February 12, 1947. It transformed fashion as it "abolished at a stroke the mannish silhouette" and revealed to the world the "New Look".[1]

Haute couture, or high fashion, today is a special designation created by the French government. To be considered haute couture, a brand must own an atelier in Paris with at least 15 full-time employees and present at least 35 looks in a show, twice a year. The list of the designers is drawn up by the Chambre Syndicale de la Haute Couture. In Parisian couture, there is a constant struggle between the creative aspect of the business and the financial. While each garment is a handmade piece of art showcasing the talents of the atelier, couture is a loss-making business in Europe. But couture is not limited to the storied French ateliers. In 1917, Cristóbal Balenciaga established his couture house in San Sebastián in Spain; in the 1950s, Azzedine Alaïa was working for couture houses in Tunis, Tunisia.

The story of Indian couture is different. Indian couture is inextricably linked to bridal couture. In the absence of high society events, gallery openings, and balls, couture is resigned to bridal or occasion wear. The statistics of the industry are mind-boggling: according to a report by KPMG in 2017, the Indian wedding industry is estimated to be around $50 billion in size[2] and is the second largest in the world.[3] The industry, however, is changing. With the upsurge in the number of millionaires by 300 per cent in Bombay and Delhi,[4] their need for couture beyond occasion wear is rising and transforming the contours

Francesco Renaldi's late 18th-century painting "Muslim Lady Reclining", features a young lady (*above*), presumed to be the wife of an English merchant living in Dhaka, wearing sheer, delicate layers atop heavy silks.

This served as inspiration for Tahiliani's romantic second dupattas to complete a modern bride's ensemble (*facing page*). The sheer veil is like a gossamer cloud or mist around the face.

Deepika Padukone is a vision in silk, *resham* and
Swarovski cabochon stones and the ever-present
ombre veil, 2007.

of the industry. Bridal couture, however, is the mainstay for Indian designers, the fodder that fuels their ready-to-wear lines—a trend opposite from that in the West. The Tahiliani studio employs 50 full-time employees in couture in its sprawling atelier in Gurgaon led by Mansha Sahni.

—

Indian couture came into its own in the 1990s at a point when Bombay society was in the grips of a new renaissance modelled on the American soap opera *The Bold and the Beautiful*. The inner circle of high society was made up of a small but formidable group of women who formed the nucleus of Tahiliani's first client list, the sort of women who ordered "white blouses for funerals" from the designer. For them, minor variations in details took on major significance where cut-throat competition pushed each client to want more. As weddings became more ostentatious so did the bridal trousseau. Tahiliani created dazzling lehengas—embroidered with drapes; with a whisper of a trail and dramatic yokes with airy *bandhani* dupattas—each skilfully tailored and distinctive for the fearsomely elegant women of the day. Adding to his list of illustrious clients were Bollywood actresses and a galaxy of Arabian princesses. As Tahiliani's star rose, his pieces were seen from Karachi to Paris; when Isabella Blow stepped out in one of his creations with the designer in tow, Tahiliani's status as a vital force in style was cemented.

Big changes in India, from liberalization to the burgeoning party scene, shook up the fashion world and the business of couture would have to adjust to changing styles and perceptions. With the launch of "Page 3" in the dailies, where society parties and upper-class soirees captured readers' attention, no bride came to embody this period more fully than Tanya Godrej. A graceful lithe woman, soft-spoken and cultured, her brief to Tahiliani was that she should be able to "dance at her wedding," recalls Dilnaz Karbhary, who handled couture. Though jewellery tends to be the final flourish to an outfit, Tahiliani designed Godrej's *jadau* choli around an incredibly large emerald Nizam pendant that adorned her neck. Intricate handwork added multi-dimensionality and there was not a drop of shine to be seen. Despite this, the piece gleamed in dull antique silver and the sweeping hip yoke lehenga was inspired by a Mughal-meets Rajput-meets-Modern vision. Suddenly, there was a new Indian vocabulary.

This was a bridal ensemble that revealed an intuitive facet of the TT woman: carefree and confident. On the night of her wedding, Godrej walked, twirled, and dipped. From then on, brides were assured lightness and instructed to just "kick and walk" because the lehenga would no longer be heavy at the ankles. Tahiliani was billed as a designer who understood the pace of a modern woman's life.

In his quest for weightlessness, Tahiliani oversaw several prototypes for the under-construction of a lehenga. The studio played with many odd shapes and strange materials, made countless versions and variations. They used bamboo to create a frame, a cage on which great swathes of fabric could be laid but it was too stiff. They studied Victorian costumes, their hooped skirts and understood the need for crinolines which could create a beautiful shape without adding bulk. Tahiliani and Ajju finally settled on a horsehair crinoline which enlarged the lehenga, gave it adequate volume while maintaining the shape and ensuring lightness.

They used devices to compress the waist, make the skirts look fuller, and help the dress project from behind. Tahiliani's work during the period changed how a woman occupied the space around her. The studio's aim was to turn exploratory thoughts into something wearable and manageable without compromising on the uniqueness of each garment and the way it was linked to the past—tradition—and the present, and how it could endure the future.

—

On a cool afternoon in Bombay, Minal Modi entered Ensemble. She had met Tahiliani at a dinner and explained her predicament. Modi had the finest French chiffon from Joel and Son in London and matching mules had been made to order by Manolo Blahnik. All she needed now was a designer to dress her for Godrej's wedding, to create something that she had been mulling over in her head. To Tahiliani, she was a rare creature, the sort of woman that zig-zagged across fashion capitals, spanning continents and collections, who sought the finest not for appearances but to satisfy a delight in dressing up.

"Drape me like a turban," she told Tahiliani. With those words, the drape series was created.

Tahiliani designed the Fluted Collection based upon her couture request. Subsequently, many of Tahiliani's iconic pieces, including the draped corset were influenced and informed by Modi's style, a nod to the myth of the artist creating in service to the muse. "She showed us a new world," recalls Ajju. Modi brought to the studio corsets from Vivienne Westwood and Vera Wang that were paired with saris in *chikan*, in *ari*, with French chiffon and hand embroidery. The corset, a remedy for shapelessness, became a focus of attraction for the studio as they attempted to replicate it. The design team's careful study of Westwood corsets, their attempt to take apart the original and search for a substitute for the boning—India did not manufacture trims nor were imports permitted—resulted in the use of *jibbi*s, plastic tongue cleaners, instead. Over the years, the corset would be skilfully cut and equipped with darts, ribs, whalebones and, above all, a drape.

The story of couture in India was thus a drama of creative survival. Tahiliani updated the measuring chart in India which previously consisted of five measurements to more than twelve. Tahiliani and Ajju studied the body of each client, figuring out ways to slim down a fuller client, to lift the bust or to straighten a hunched back. There was always the struggle to make something original, and the evolution of the lehenga from looking like a tent to a slimming lehenga with a long trail, followed by the mermaid lehenga were all a means to remain relevant in the world of fashion.

By the time Tahiliani settled into his studio in Delhi, he was recognized as one of the premier dressmakers to the rich and famous, designing pieces for a clientele that could afford his perfectionism, craftmanship, and the clothes for a life well lived.

—

Tahiliani is an art buff, able to hold his ground on old-master drawings and sculptures with equal ease. He seldom passes an opportunity to explore a new exhibit and it was on one such visit to New York's Metropolitan Museum of Art in 1985 where he came across the "Costumes of Royal India". A walk around the rooms that housed 140 mannequins in court costumes lent by the former ruling families of Indian princely states displayed white muslins and glowing colours of silk brocades that showcased the splendour of the past. That afternoon stayed with him for almost two decades.

Tahiliani paid homage to this idea in 2008 with a novel experience at the Bridal Couture Exposition. Titled "The Procession", it opened to customers and visitors an immersive world where he introduced important trends for the seasons, bringing together couture, wedding, and art. In its third year, he showcased "The Artisan", a tribute to craftsmanship and the people who had revived and invigorated finery from *zardozi* to *dabka*. It was a celebration of surface embellishment paralleling the level of Mughal-era artistry.

Each year was an overload of opulence where the pieces beckoned: come closer. The expositions were an invitation to a dialogue on dress. In Tahiliani's pieces, there was a sharpness of cut juxtaposed with the softness of drape. There was a sunburst of embroidery, trellises were decorated with pink roses and the big story was brocade, which gave shimmer and texture. There was a bevy of embroidered flowers, and hand-woven stitches done as per the needs and desires of clients. The couture collections allowed Tahiliani to reach further and deeper into history, from ancient to modern and, on the brides, he recalled a grandeur of the past.

In 2014, at the newly instituted Indian Bridal Week, Tahiliani introduced the Modern Mughals, a synthesis of traditional styles and modern tailoring. Male models walked in kurtas, sherwanis, jodhpurs, and pre-draped dhotis with cummerbunds in a collaboration with Savile Row's Whitcomb and Shaftesbury.

—

The atelier with its reputation of excellence has dressed some of the biggest names from Bombay to Dubai. When in 2009, Shilpa Shetty approached Tahiliani to design her wedding outfit, the designer was in the throes of a rejuvenation, at a time when the idea for India Modern was crystallizing into a codified vision. Shetty's wedding outfit encapsulated the idea. Shetty, a Tuluva from Mangalore, was marrying a Punjabi and wanted her wedding outfit to be a celebration of not just their union but a coming together of cultures. Tahiliani used the lehenga as a starting point and incorporated a sari drape, in a first for the studio. Pleats were made of silk brocade while the drape was done in Italian tulle. The blouse was soldered in tiny Swarovski crystals and outlined with *kasab* and had a traditional *zardozi* and *kundan-jadau* border. The challenge was to ensure the embroidery was light enough to be moulded. Fifteen embroiderers worked for 15 days on the piece that weighed less than 3 kilos.

In a world where everything is visible, that which is left unsaid is almost magical. Deep inside Gurgaon, in a red brick structure, is Tahiliani's design atelier. Every day hundreds of people filter in, a fashion army of design heads, samplers, pattern cutters, tailors, embroiders, and seamstresses.

An outfit starts on Tahiliani's table, an organized chaos of stacks of swatches and colourful pencils that create detailed sketches of immaculately dressed women with elongated heads that are at once surreal and beautiful. A couture commission moves from department to department, seeking the right colour, to the table of the cutter, to the floor with the embroiderers who work to loud sounds of *qawwali*, across the atrium and its constant hum of sewing machines, to the chatter of the women who labour over beads to make the tassels. Last but not least, a seamstress sews on the hook that will hold it all up. It is they who transform a sketch into a showpiece of luxury. The number of hours spent on one piece are illustrative of a discipline that is seldom captured in these Instagram-driven times.

The result is a couture creation that is at once a public performance and an intimate conversation between the House of Tahiliani and the person for whom it was made.

Long before others, Tahiliani used striking older women in his campaigns. The idea was to portray a begum, a matriarch sitting amongst other women of her family wearing the latest designs using different colours and techniques of the season.
FESTIVE BRIDAL 2010

Detailed drawings of
outfits are made for
couture clients once they
choose the panels. These
drawings help the clients
visualize what the final
garment will look like.

FACING PAGE: Jewel
percussion lehenga.
BRIDAL & COUTURE 2013

Once completed, all garments are photographed on mannequins both to send to the client and for documentation.

Models in swirls of red brocade cholis with draped hip yokes on lehengas, evoking memories of an era gone by.
BRIDAL & COUTURE 2016

A stunning, one
of-a-kind *zardozi*
embroidered veil.
To add to its richness
are hair jewels akin to
those worn by Indian
classical dancers. This
particular panelled veil
has an embroidered
parandi added to give
a graded jewel effect.
BRIDAL & COUTURE 2018

Shot at Jaipur's iconic Gem Palace, these images recall old-world Rajputana glamour. Models wear dupattas accentuated with custom three-dimensional *gotta patti* flowers, 2019.

Lisa Haydon looking
resplendent in "Moon
Dust"—a delicately
romantic take on a
cocktail sari embellished
with Swarovski elements
and a hand-embroidered
thread-work border.
BRIDAL & COUTURE 2011

"DRAPE—OUTLINING CURVING LINES, CONTOURING THE SHAPE OF THE BODY."

TARUN TAHILIANI

Inspired by the elegant carriage of the flamingo, a blush pink lehenga skirt with sheer silk folds uplifted with Swarovski crystals, paired with a hazy tulle dupatta, 2015.

Opposites attract: a lehenga need not always be matched with a formal "blouse". As seen here, an appliqué organza lehenga skirt paired with a minutely encrusted bodysuit and sheer Italian tulle.
BRIDAL & COUTURE 2016

FACING PAGE: First made famous by Christian Dior in the 1940s, the peplum is a silhouette for the sophisticated. Seen here is Tahiliani's version called the Chandrabala design, which is a panelled peplum bodice in silk thread embroidery worn with a panelled lehenga and a veil.

A tableau of fine *chikankari* that has saris and *anarkalis*, with sheer sleeves and infused with *gotta patti*.
BRIDAL & COUTURE 2016

GOTTA + CRYSTAL

The weight of a garment for festive and bridal Indian clothing is a major challenge to overcome. *Gotta patti* scores because it is rich, traditional and light. Soldered crystal has the same effect—fused together they create weightlessness, depth, and dazzle.

FACING PAGE: A gift from Awadh, *chikankari* finds many iterations in the house's vocabulary.

A touch whimsy, graceful splatter of *gotta* work on Italian tulle, finished with hand embroidery.

This pearl encrusted
sleeve ensemble with
floral *gotta patti* work
was inspired by the
ornate ceiling of the
Shrine of Imam Reza
in Mashhad, Iran that
Tahiliani visited in 2016.

LIGHTNESS

"For years, I have seen brides who can barely move or walk on their wedding day. They are left scratched and bruised from their bridal finery. Luxury has to be first about how you feel in it and on your skin. We have always tried to make clothes lighter so that they feel beautiful on the skin rather than seems beautiful only in the way they are worn. We achieve lightness making breakthroughs in fabric, construction, and techniques."

BRIDAL & COUTURE 2018

The Tarakanna
Collection shows
different silhouettes
embroidered with
gotta, *sitara* and
Swarovski crystals.
BRIDAL & COUTURE 2016

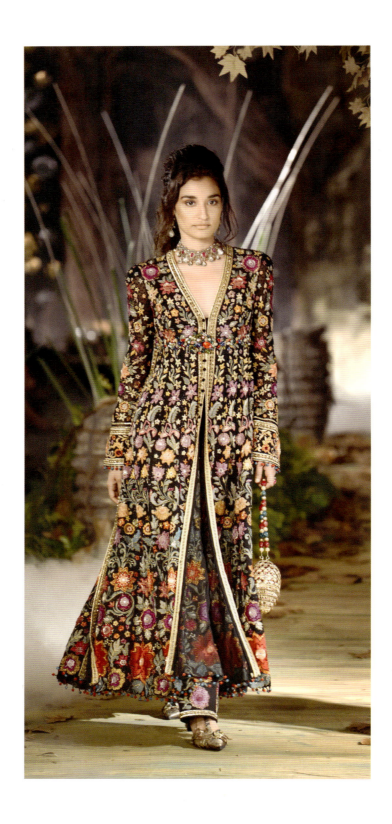

GARA

Gara is fine thread-work embroidery predominantly worn by the Parsi community. The style of embroidery was brought to India by the Parsis who adopted this from the Chinese with whom they traded in tea, cotton, and opium. The word *gara* comes from the Gujarati word *garo*—meaning width. This new kind of embroidery showed realistic depictions of flora and fauna and Oriental scenes. Like many art techniques, *gara* embroidery over time evolved with Indian designers and craftsmen adopting it on modern silhouettes.

The Autumn/Winter 2017 Collection references the Parsi *gara* embroidery with additions of French knots and *aari* embroidery. "No Parsi *gara* piece is complete without the famed cranes in flight. Because I started my career in fashion in Mumbai, I was exposed to Parsi women wearing exquisite saris with *gara* embroidery very early on in my career. I would buy old borders with *gara* embroidery and use them on silk coats with slip kurtas to create fluid and weightless elegance."

An underwater palette
evoking fantastical
visions of the mysterious
marine life in sea-green.
BRIDAL & COUTURE 2019

FACING PAGE: A sleek,
body-hugging pistachio
ensemble sheathed in
mukaish work paired
with a custom-cut
slim dupatta.
BRIDAL & COUTURE 2018

SURFACE SOLDER

Traditionally, *mukaish* was used extensively in *chikankari* to add embellishments to the garments. Over a period of time designers began to create entire pieces with only *mukaish* work because of its delicacy and glamour. As raw material for *mukaish* became coarser, tiny crystals were substituted to create a similar twinkling effect. The sari and bodice on the following page are fine examples of this.

MUKAISH

Thousands of fine-as-fibre metal threads are twisted and
pressed individually to create floral motifs and dots in
metal for *mukaish* work, also known as *badla* or *kamdani*.

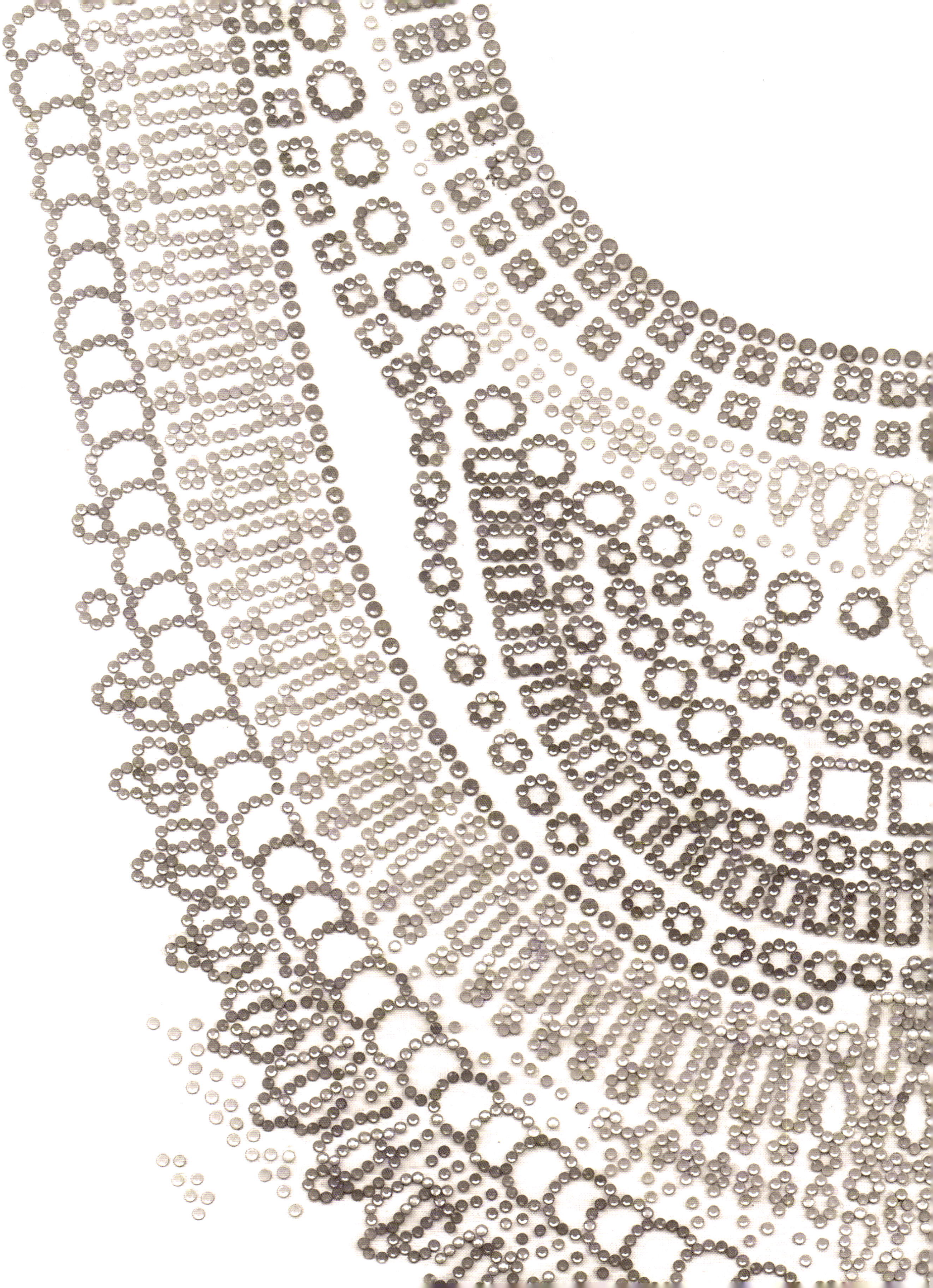

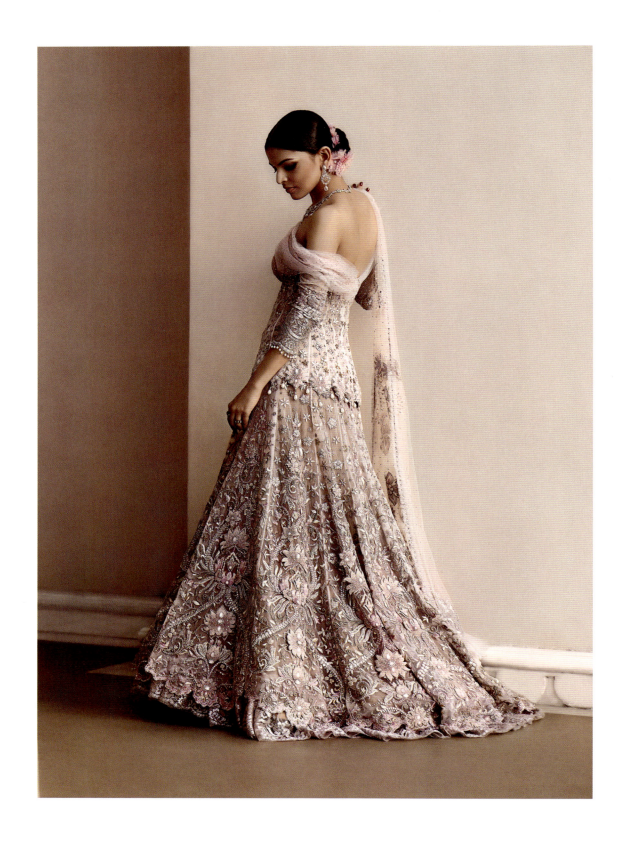

FRENCH KNOTS, 3D FLOWERS, SPRAYS AND MORE

French knots are hand-embroidered decorative stitches made by winding threads one or multiple times and knotting them together. 3D flowers are hand cut and hand embroidered. They are usually embellished to give the effect of real flowers with dew drops. This lehenga gives the illusion of an evening gown. With a structured drape, it has silk thread work done using extensive techniques and 3D flowers in graded French knots for size and tonality. Sprays, marquee-shaped stones, and a variety of other materials have been hand-sewn onto this scalloped-edged lehenga.

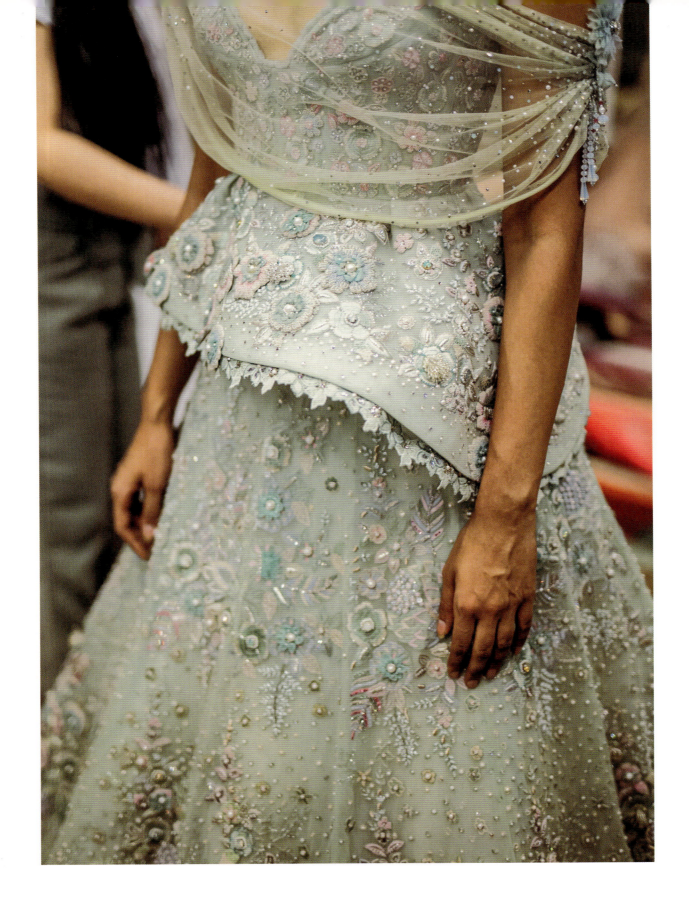

WEIGHTLESSNESS

"The floral 'Bloom' lehenga with a structured drape. As women want more volume, we have to find ways to balance the weight. This is done by using fine silk threads that are enhanced with French knots and tiny coloured crystals soldered on. We work hard to achieve this weightlessness in our pieces so that they are easy to wear and comfortable, such as this floral 'Bloom' lehenga with a structured drape on the facing page." COUTURE 2019

Embroidered dupattas
are increasingly seen as
cumbersome because of
their width and weight.
A structured drap or
wings that attach and
snap on the shoulders
are preferred thereby
allowing the hands
more movement.

Fitting the "Bloom" lehenga on model-musician Kavya Trehan.
BRIDAL & COUTURE 2019 | BLOOM

"How much more love can be lavished on these individual couture pieces by the hands of our craftsmen?"

TARUN TAHILIANI

KASHIDA MODERN

One of the oldest forms of embroidery known to Indians, *kashida* originates in Kashmir. With signature floral motifs and a focus on paisley, this collection is an ode to Tahiliani's deep commitment to collecting and continuing to showcase this exquisite needle work from Kashmir. Well-known actress Kriti Sanon in a multicoloured, pearl and *zardozi* embroidered "*Kashida*" lehenga.

"A coat, draped bustier and pants in *kashida* embroidery worn with Byzantium buckles. Women today want to use their clothes differently—and the crop top, trousers or lehenga is an increasingly popular silhouette. The coat adds formality, and the umbrella with antique embroidery shows a connection to the past. While I have always loved the gold bullion work on the *zardozi* such as displayed on the umbrella, I feel that in modern wear it is cumbersome and heavy. We have developed our *kashida* versions so that the fabric can mould and drape to the body and still have this exquisite Indian richness."

This 18-*kali* Pichwai
lehenga features
monochromatic scenes
featuring typical motifs
such as birds, animals,
plants, and flowers.
The Pichwai Collection
was created under the
silence of the forced
lockdown during the
COVID-19 pandemic.
The collection reflects
the mood—simple,
monochromatic, quiet,
using all the symbolism
associated with
this tradition.

CHIKAN MODERN

Chikankari is the "lace of India". It moulds the body, is never abrasive, and the *jaali* ventilates the skin. This style of embroidery was believed to be popularized and patronized by Mughal empress Noor Jahan (1577–1645, wife of emperor Jehangir), the great tastemaker who was also a fine embroideress herself. *Chikankari* gets modified but remains a staple at the Tahiliani studio.

Sculpted lace and sequins caress the body in an almost imperceptibly sheer neckline that ends in soft wings over a lehenga.

"The TT logo resembles pi,
thus representing infinite possibilities."

TARUN TAHILIANI

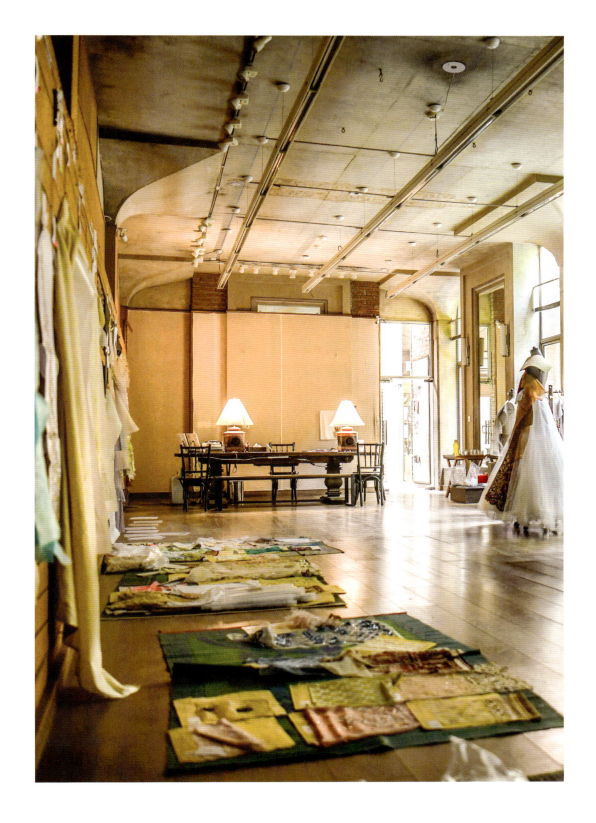

A FORTRESS AND A SANCTUARY

"Stephane Paumier was designing my studio when he talked about his idea of using cement concrete and using the domes of the tombs of Delhi in a modern way. I was super excited. I had just come back from Istanbul where the work of the architect Philip De Campo was on display on how you play with natural light so that it makes patterns inside the building all day. A lot of our rooms are filled with natural light. He has designed for me a building that I bless him for every day when I am here at work."

Images of the
atelier from the
25th anniversary
celebration, 2020.

"In contrast to the majority of fashion traditions worldwide, Indian designers heavily depend on the artistic skills and manual craftsmanship of their *karigars*. They employ techniques that have been passed down through generations, akin to cherished folktales, blending tradition with contemporary interpretation. Operating in multiple realms, they serve as the backbone for Indian designers, acting as the scaffold that elevates their creations. It is essential to recognize them as artisans rather than mere labourers, and to appreciate the immense possibilities they bring forth... we are indebted to them."

12

A NEW INDEPENDENCE

BORN OF TECHNIQUES AND EXPERIENCE

"The hours of folly are measur'd by the clock, but of wisdom: no clock can measure."

WILLIAM BLAKE

The year was 2020 and it began with carefree abandonment. It was going to be a year of celebrations and festivities, of pomp and party.

For Tahiliani, it was also a year of study. He was immersed in his archives, sorting through years of sketches, some in organized folders, others in a stack of leather-bound notebooks. He studied his own evolution—how a trouser suit transformed into a draped jumpsuit, or how the heavily embroidered lehenga was developed into a hand painted digitized version, weightless with bursts of embroidery. Not one collection was spared. Each piece was scrutinized. How could a style be updated? What new materials and techniques could be incorporated? The studio worked together putting into practice what the House of Tahiliani learnt over all these years. For the 25 Year Collection, we decided to bring some of the best techniques that the studio had worked on and integrate them together. Painting, *kashida* embroidery, draping—taking elements from different collections and synthesizing them further—it is through this connection that some of these pieces were made, drawing on techniques honed over several years.

They began with the mother-of-pearl blouse that Sal wore to Tina Tahiliani's wedding in 1990. It was a radical idea for its time, set to look like an encrusted pearls rather than the oft-seen sheeted sequins or *zardozi*. For the 25 Year Collection, the intention was to enhance it further so that it looked like nothing short of jewellery. They refined the design by adding cabochons, Swarovski crystals, half-round pearls, buttons, and topped it off with ostrich feathers. It was paired with a classical *jamdani*, a pearly textile for a touch of sophisticated elegance.

It was also a year of reunions. Returning to the studio after two decades was Anupama Kabra who had worked with Tahiliani on his first show at Dorchester in London in 1994. Unlike the embroidered original, Kabra hand-painted the textiles in shades of old rose and jade with a touch of gold and sky blue. It was then digitized and delicately embroidered. Tahiliani had never been comfortable with a fully embroidered ensemble since it compromised the drape often using digital printing as the basis of his artwork. The truest illustration was the jade *jamawar* coat from the anniversary edition.

"Weightless and soft," Tahiliani said, again and again to each piece. There they were: a shawl as a jade *jamawar* coat, lehengas, and many pieces in brocade. Fluted saris were sculpted further. When they shot it, Lakshmi Rana wore a T-shirt from the Milan Collection with a brocade cocoon coat and salwar trousers. The looks were a testament to the lessons learnt at the House of Tahiliani. When they were unveiled, it was a night of triumph that began with a celebration. Models, editors, photographers, and friends took an evening stroll around the Qutub Minar serenaded by qawwals reminiscent of the magic of a bygone era, lost sometime in 1193. Twenty-five years synthesized into one moment by those who know it best—Gautam Kalra styled this anniversary collection while Tarun Vishwa photographed it. The clothes and jewellery were handed to them and they worked their magic to conceptualise and execute the entire 25th anniversary shoot.

It was also a year for fashion as art. Unlike with his previous collections, Tahiliani had the freedom to create away from commercial constraints. "When one switches to a marketing world that is driven by creating need rather than addressing a need, the whole mechanism is developed for the mall, the big brand, the fashion show. A whole generation has gone by since advertizing and marketing became really powerful. You didn't even understand how you were being fed. A fashion system that is fuelled by a desire to grow with a board of directors isn't looking for magic. They see magic as only one thing, sales up from 15 per cent to 40," he said as the House of Tahiliani charged ahead.

But such is the folly of time, it has different plans. And so in 2020, overnight, life as we knew it was put on hold.

—

Much like the rest of India, Tahiliani was glued to the screen on March 23rd, 2020, in anticipation of Prime Minister Modi's big announcement on the pandemic. With the country shutting down at four hours' notice, with a lack of guidelines, people retreated into their homes. Tahiliani was amidst a great season. The stores were filled with stock from the spring collection that had been reordered while the studio was busy planning for fall. Fabric had been ordered for 10,000 pieces that would be shown at the five stores, boutiques, and e-commerce websites. Though nothing was cut or dyed, the studio was operating at full capacity.

When all this came to a screeching halt, the first cry came from anxious brides. For his part, despite the initial shock, Tahiliani was at peace. Away from the tedium of a calendar, he embraced the forced independence. He sketched and drew. Rather than to meet the needs of his brides or the demands of the business, this was fashion as art and art as escape.

"As I'd been already thinking, with the book and the pieces, they rekindled those old moments. Where did life go? Where did those twenty years go? Where did I go? It was a recentring and it was long overdue. The pandemic was a catalyst that just sped up the process. I couldn't have stayed distracted for much longer," he says.

Tahiliani settled into his home office in Delhi, a tranquil space nestled amidst a cocoon of plants at their farmhouse. He worked under a glass and steel shark sculpture. It was a world contained in itself with a Figurettes body form, treadmill, books, and curious objets d'art. With the city under complete lockdown, Tahiliani absorbed a silence he'd seldom experienced.

"I thought, if the business shuts down, it shuts down. We will start over."

"A strange disquiet," he called it with bird songs and little else. That was until the howl. Overnight, migrant workers, daily-wage labourers from New Delhi to Bombay, took to the streets. Ordinarily invisible, the army of hungry workers poured out. With the doors to his factory shut, queues of workers from the surrounding industrial complex gathered in search for food. Tahiliani with two other companies in Gurgaon began to feed 1,000 workers.

"It was a drop in the ocean, but it was path altering. Seeing the whole mass migration, how people were desperate for work—you don't confront these things normally. People begging outside your factory for food. These are people who are working with dignity. They were not beggars.

It definitely changed my engagement, perception, and empathy and therefore what drives me," he says.

Fashion as a fraternity responded in unison. Newspapers carried pieces of fashion's COVID Patient No. 1 from the recently concluded Paris Fashion Week, websites suggested the cosiest looks for work-from-home and editors replaced their glossy airbrushed covers with pristine images of nature. A big debate raged: Was this the big reset? Was this the rewriting of old norms of production and consumption?

—

This pandemic like all pandemics can have a correctional effect. Indeed, as Arundathi Roy writes, "Historically, pandemics have forced humans to break with the past and imagine their world anew. This one is no different. It is a portal, a gateway between one world and the next."

Much like the Black Death in the 14th century, COVID-19 too could allow workers greater bargaining powers and ensure greater agency to the underprivileged. Tahiliani supported this. As in with *chikan* where artisans worked from their villages, so too could the Bengali, UP and Uttarakhand artisans. Meanwhile, fear and uncertainty plagued workers and businesses. With vague rules and incoherent policies, migrant workers began their long march to the security of their homes. Contractual labour sensing an impending doom followed suit. With the factory shut, many workers at Tahiliani's studio too began their journey home. Embroiders, pattern cutters, and workers from the factory returned to their villages. When Tahiliani finally ventured out to get his cheque book to pay salaries, he saw a ghost town, not a city.

As soon as the lockdown was lifted, when Tahiliani first opened the doors to the factory, he didn't know how many people would return. They began work on the *pichwai*, ivory and weightless. "We started in a panic with a very sketchy staff. For a little while whoever wanted work worked. We concocted things and just gave it to them," he recalls.

Four months into the pandemic, in a world transformed by digital modes of communication, Tahiliani hosted India's first digital full-length Instagram fashion show called "Pieces of You" from the mood board room in his studio in Gurgaon. Models walked in crinkles in bright colours and Grecian fluting to an audience that logged in from across India, Dubai, and Tanzania.

Behind the scenes, the team worked with mechanical precision. Tahiliani, his designers, assistants, and light men were in hazmat suits and double masked. Models were assigned separate rooms, and no one was allowed to share water bottles. Everything was pre-labelled. Nobody was allowed movement in and out except for the models.

"It was intense, like being in an operation theatre from where these gilded swans came floating out. Surreal," he says.

With messages and hearts popping up from Mehr Jesia to Tina Tahiliani, the show itself was a reprieve in lonely times allowing for a little connection during isolation and ultimately a testament to Tahiliani's belief that fashion ought to bring us all a little closer, from India's first ever fashion show in Ensemble to India's first ever full-length digital fashion show.

As for sales, though they made a full collection, the business survived by sending samples to different parts of the country unlike the norm where each store has its own sample. Historically, during times of conflict, as it was in February 1943 during the Second World War, fashion never stopped. While some couturiers fell out of business others continued to show collections despite the reduction in the number of models in Paris from 100 to 60. Tahiliani's collection too shrunk rising by about 70 per cent in 2022.

—

Rebuilding the team after the initial shock took almost nine months. The studio was short staffed, pushing and pulling and reallocating. The embroidery strength never returned to pre-pandemic levels but that's because Tahiliani kept his promise. He began sending work to the artisans in their villages where they could work from the security of their homes. He found ways to work with dyers in Rajkot, Jamnagar, and Bhuj without uprooting them.

With plume and colourful stones, a standout sequinned blouse is complimented by a shimmering silver concept sari.
25 YEAR COLLECTION 2020

PRINT ON
DUPION
OR
NET
OR
SHANTUNG
SLIGHT TIG

a month, with little success at the craft bazaars. COVID-19 worsened a deteriorating situation where mill-made fabric gained hegemony over handloom. But Tahiliani stood his ground. With the launch of Taasva, his menswear label in collaboration with Aditya Birla Fashion, Tahiliani pushed for working with weavers from Benaras. While there was a presence of blended fabrics with viscose at the new label, Tahiliani insisted they work with weavers and not the giant Chinese looms in Surat that have the capacity to churn at industrial speed. In the end, the weavers delivered 40-50,000 meters of cloth.

George Birdwood, the Anglo-Indian writer and naturalist, writing in 1880, noted that the craft practice of Indian artisans was based on the "tradition of a system of decoration founded on perfect principles, which they have learned through centuries of practice to apply with unerring truth."[1] This continues to hold relevance for India where craft is not a thing of the past, but a thing of the present as well as of the future. With nearly twenty-three million crafts persons still practicing, craft is as contemporary as mass production and has great social and economical potential in the mechanized world of the future.

Tahiliani has risen to the occasion, citing often that embroidery today parallels that of the Mughal period. But the number of artisans are dwindling as handloom villages from Benaras to Bengal wind down their generations-old practices for daily-wage labour.

"Maybe these things weren't so important to me before, but they are so important to me now. We think that we will use a particular foil jersey or a crinkle only because we can't get it in India. So now, as a design house, it's not that I won't use things from abroad because the stones come from abroad, but I'm committed to first looking at what we can do here," he says.

This belief has pushed Tahiliani to explore textiles further, to devise methods to manipulate handloom, to treat it. "I had stopped handloom. Traditionally, they like it to look big and stiff and they gum fabrics and calendar. There are many techniques to make it heavier, stiffer, to give it volume. I like the opposite. I like a thicker fabric that can drape like a jersey," says Tahiliani. Tahiliani is thus seeking heavier weaves and learning new ways to treat them so that something as prosaic as khadi can feel exquisite.

"We got too spoilt, having everything at our beck and call. The pandemic forced us to have greater thought and planning," says Tahiliani.

The pandemic also pushed Tahiliani further towards the weavers. For years, he saw them struggle to sell three saris

Brocade—beyond saris and lehengas.

Lakshmi Rana wears a three-piece concept sari with an appliqué bustier made using boning and a permanently pleated crushed sari drape from which emanates a sheer black organza *pallu* that, because of the wiring, sits like a halo around the head.

This is a take on the typical classical Mughal look of sheer tissue worn over brocades. However, in the modern avatar, this is done with embroidered pants ornamented with tiny pearls and crystals so it sparkles through. On it, the model is wearing a very fine gold tulle skirt, cut in panels as done by the Mughals.

25 YEAR COLLECTION 2020

Orange organza and feathered wisp of fabric were techniques first used in the Kumbhback Collection of 2013. "The visit to Kumbh was fresh in our minds when we created this outfit that includes *kashida* work, making it a Kumbh-meets-Rabari inspired design. The bright colours of Kumbh, combined with the mirror work and *jadau* choli created a fun, funky lehenga."
25 YEAR COLLECTION 2020

A gold foil drape based
on the dhoti worn
with a choli gilet with
Byzantium motifs from
the Tahiliani archives.
25 YEAR COLLECTION 2020

> *"I am no longer thinking, this is India, this is Kutch.*
> *It's a visceral process that has come together and*
> *that's how I want to design. I don't want a theme."*

TARUN TAHILIANI

During the lockdown, with time on his side, Tahiliani also began experimenting. He built a mud pit in his backyard and, forever fascinated with the Indian patina—the shades of ageing and dust—he studied manners in which clothes could be aged. When he got a Bengali khadi he loved, he buried it in the pit. This piece went on to be added to his first physical campaign since the pandemic began at the very last minute.

—

Two years into the pandemic, Tahiliani returned with pieces so powerful as though the pandemic had left no dent. There was the *pichwai* lehenga, hand painted and embroidered in tone-on-tone silk threads and pearls with a touch of *navratna* stones topped with a French lace blouse that had a plunging neckline. He took this further when he opened Couture Week in July 2022.

The show itself, on July 2022 in New Delhi, was unlike the hyper staged drama of yesteryears in large auditoriums. The collection was unveiled in an intimate ballroom with friends, buyers, and the press, reminiscent of the earlier Dior and Alaia shows. Though it was couture, the traditional stopped bride was replaced by a modern woman who held a short veil in her hand, confirming Tahiliani's desire to have the veil emancipate rather than weigh a woman down.

In the couture, there were hints of *prêt*. An ivory-coloured draped concept sari in a foiled jersey merged with a corset blouse encrusted in diamonds. It was high fashion that was also ready to wear. There was a mix of styles and influences.

"I am no longer thinking, this is India, this is Kutch. It's a visceral process that has come together and that's how I want to design. I don't want a theme. What can India be? How can it have a theme when you come from something

that is so layered, is so old, and has so many million influences. What theme can encapsulate that?" he asked.

India is a feeling, it is a sense of independence and perhaps it took a pandemic for Tahiliani to embrace that. In 2022, Tahiliani played with the fashion calendar, finishing the sketches for his spring collection to show them in October. He planned on launching Spring/Summer later because in India, the seasons turn later. "We don't have to follow the Western calendar," he said. By 2023, Tahiliani returned to his 2011–2012 archives in a bid to further *prêt*. Rinkal Sharma, who heads *prêt*, attempted to modernize the body hugging and loser drapery. "Tarun wanted it cool," she said. Indeed, his preoccupation was how the sari would appeal to the youth.

While ready-to-wear casual clothing, the ubiquitous presence of jeans, jeggings, and trackpants in the Indian woman's wardrobe, has transformed a land of sensuous drapery, Tahiliani marvels at how saris are still his second-best seller. But he has plans.

"Imagine I cut a dhoti-sari just under the knee and pair it with a button-down shirt in cotton with a collar. That's where my head is going. I think the top Indian designers became India decoration and there is no modernity. What we are trying to do is to relook at all these things and our classics and trying to make them more accessible. Fashion can't be sold just to the super rich. It also has to find a younger voice that starts to interpret it in their way. We have to provide Indian answers and Indian solutions," he says.

This then is the path on a journey, an idea known as India Modern, and leading the way is Tahiliani, a traveller, truthseeker, and designer. As for the dazzling garments he makes along the way, those remain in tribute to that which has forever inspired him: his land and its people: untouched, unaffected, and unapologetically Indian.

A classic sherwani and pleated stole over our trademark dhoti that is clinched with the cummerband, normally worn on top—a new modern way.

FACING PAGE: The evolution of the draped concept sari with one embroidered tulle wing and a slightly scattered corset.

Lavender signature concept sari, with a stylized Swarovski encrusted bodysuit draped in a delicate tulle fabric embroidered with sequins and crystals, detailed with lace.

The seven-piece groom set consisting of a sherwani, kurta, churidar, stole, safa, fabric jutti, and cummerbund. The tone-on-tone jacquard sherwani is embroidered in dori threadwork. Featuring motifs inspired by Mughal architecture, it is paired with a raw silk kurta, a stretch poplin churidar, and a chanderi safa.

"DRAPERY, LIGHTNESS, TRADITION, CRAFT, AND FREEDOM— THIS IS INDIA MODERN."

TARUN TAHILIANI

Notes

EARLY YEARS

1. Henry McGee. "Interview with Ritu Kumar." *Creating Emerging Markets Oral History Collection*, Harvard Business School, January 14, 2015.

2. S. Mehta, "The Day of the Designer," *Bombay*, December 22, 1988, pp. 70–76.

3. Ibid.

4. B. Crossette, "India allows Pepsi in after 2-year debate," Section D, *The New York Times*, September 20, 1988, p. 5.

NEW LINES—NEW TECHNIQUES

1. A. Kabra, "Tarun Tahiliani presents his Rubaiyat." Jury interview for a dissertation, National Institute for Design, 1995.

2. S. Abraham, "The heterotopic space of Chirag Delhi." B. Arch Dissertation, 2012–2013.

3. Toolika Gupta, "The Effect of British Raj on Indian Costume." 2011.

4. S. Chatterjee and R. Mohan. "India's Garment Exports." *Economic and Political Weekly*, August 1993.

5. T. Singh, "National Institute of Fashion Technology plans to provide facilities unavailable in India." *India Today*, November 1986.

6. Barbara Crossette, "New Fashion School in India Draws from A Rick Heritage." *The New York Times*, 21 June 1989.

JOURNEY TO INDIA MODERN

1. Bishnupriya Gupta, "Competition and Control in the Market for Textiles: Indian Weavers and the English East India Company in the 18th Century." In Giorgio Riello and Tirthankar Roy (Eds.), *How India Clothes the World: The World of South Asian Textiles 1500-1850*. Leiden, Boston: Brill (2013), pp. 281–305.

2. Blake Smith, "Fast fashion was inspired by Europe's inability to mimic Indian garb," *Quartz India*, November 5, 2017.

3. Ibid.

4. Cybèle Gontar, "Les monuments d'Egypte." In *Heilbrunn Timeline of Art History*. New York: The Metropolitan Museum of Art, October, 2004. Available at: http://www.metmuseum.org/toah/hd/empr/hd_empr.htm (accessed March 14, 2023).

5. E.J. Hobsbawm, "Introduction: Inventing Traditions." In E.J. Hobsbawm & T.O. Ranger (Eds.), *The Invention of Tradition*, Cambridge: Cambridge University Press (1983).

6. Loubna H. Skalli, *Through a Local Prism: Gender, Globalisation and Identity in Moroccan Women's Magazines*. Lanham, MD and Oxford: Lexington Books (2006).

7. E. Wilson, "Hello, customers. Are you out there?" *The New York Times*, October, 2008.

THE NEW MAN

1. Toolika Gupta, "The influence of British rule on elite Indian menswear: the birth of the Sherwani" (PhD thesis, University of Glasgow, 2016).

2. Dipesh Chakrabarty, "Clothing the political man: a reading of the use of khadi/white in Indian public life," *Postcolonial Studies*, vol. 4, no. 1 (2001): pp. 27–38.

3. Ruchir Sharma, "Golden era of high economic growth is over," *The Economic Times*, November 3, 2008.

4. Ministry of Textiles, Government of India, *Annual Report* 2003–04.

BRIDAL & COUTURE

1. Farid Chenoune, *Dior*. New York: Assouline Publishing (2007).

2. Sanna Vohra, "India's big fat wedding industry is slowdown-proof," *Mint*, January 30, 2020.

3. Virendra Pandit, "Big Fat Indian wedding market has foreign 'suitor' Zankyou lining up," *Hindu Business Line*, April 7, 2017.

4. Manu Balachandran, "Want to be a millionaire in India? Move to Mumbai or Delhi," *Quartz India*, January 21, 2016.

A NEW INDEPENDENCE

1. George C.M. Birdwood, *The Arts of India*. Calcutta: Rupa & Co. (1988 [1880]).

References

THE CONCEPT SARI

Chishti, Rta Kapur. *Saris: Tradition and Beyond*. Edited by Martand Singh. New Delhi: Roli Books/Lustre Press, 2010.

Gandhi, Shweta. "7 sari styles for women who can't drape the six yard staple." *VOGUE*, 20 March 2019. Available at: https://www.vogue.in/content/sari-styles-for-girls-who-cant-drape-a-sari (accessed March 14, 2023).

Grobe Max. "Decoding the Great Fashion Silhouettes of Our Time." *HIGHSNOBIETY*, 2019. Available at: https://www.highsnobiety.com/p/fashion-silhouettes/ (accessed March 14, 2023).

Jay, Phyllida. *Inspired by India: How India Transformed Global Design*. New Delhi: Roli Books/Lustre Press, 2022.

Kaul, Mayank Mansingh (ed.). "Cloth and India: 1947-2015," *MARG, A Magazine of the Arts* 67, no. 4 (June-September 2016).

Rathi, Nandini. "Why the story of the sari is as complex as its pleats." *The Indian Express*. 19 February 2018. Available at: https://indianexpress.com/article/lifestyle/why-the-story-of-the-sari-is-as-complex-as-its-pleats-5066402/ (accessed March 14, 2023).

Sippy, Sujata Assomull. "A Stitch in Time: And what it means for the contemporary sari." *OPEN*, 18 October 2013. Available at: https://openthemagazine.com/features/living/a-stitch-in-time/ (accessed March 14, 2023).

Snodgrass, Mary Ellen. *World Clothing and Fashion: An Encyclopedia of History, Culture, and Social Influence* Volumes 1–2. London and New York: Routledge Taylor and Francis Group, 2015, p. 326.

"The history of sari: The nine yard wonder." *The Times of India*, 24 July 2019. Available at: https://timesofindia.indiatimes.com/life-style/fashion/buzz/the-history-of-sari-the-nine-yard-wonder/articleshow/70277974.cms (accessed March 14, 2023).

"Sari," *Oxford Learner's Dictionary*. Available at: https://www.oxfordlearnersdictionaries.com/definition/american_english/sari (accessed March 14, 2023).

Glossary

ABHA: A traditional long frock worn by Memon women in Kutch.

ACHKAN: Long coat derived from the *angrakha* with panels on the front and back with full sleeves. The front panels overlap and are secured by buttons in the centre from neckline to the waist.

AJRAK: Translated from Arabic, the word *ajrak* means blue. It is a unique form of block printing that originated in Sindh.

ANARKALI: Dress-like garment in which the bodice is cinched just below the chest and the rest of the frock is flowing, usually until the knee.

ANGRAKHA: Long collarless tunic-like garment with panels that are tied to each other in the centre front at the waistline.

ARI: Derived from the Hindi word meaning 'hook,' *ari* embroidery is a style of chain stitch.

B

BAADLA: Embroidery done with metallic threads, it can be used to give the appearance of sequin work.

BANDHANI: One of the earliest forms of surface decoration using dyes on textiles, it is a type of tie-dye textile decorated by plucking the cloth with the fingernails.

BANDHGALA: Jodhpuri suit—formal evening wear with a coat, trouser and can be accompanied by a vest.

BUNDI: Front-buttoned, hip-length sleeveless vest.

BUTTI: Small design of a single flower or motif scattered on a fabric.

BAJUBAND: armlet

C

CHANDERI: Textured handwoven saris in cotton and silk decorated with fine *zari* work.

CHAPPALS: Pair of slippers.

CHIKANKARI/CHIKAN: White-on-white embroidery where the type of stitching used depends on the specialty of the region and the type and size of the motifs. Some popular stitches include the backstitch, chain stitch and hemstitch.

CHOLI: Tight-fitting blouse that often leaves the midriff bare and is worn under the sari or with a lehenga.

CHURIDAR: Variant of the salwar, it is a pant that tapers into a tight fit at the calf and ankle.

D

DABKA: Technique used to create intricate patterns with a coiled wire which resembles a spring.

DARZI: Tailor.

DHOLAK: A traditional percussion instrument, used widely in northern India.

DHOTI: Loose cloth wrapped around the lower half of the body, passed between the legs and tucked in at the waistline.

DUPATTA: Shawl-like scarf arranged in two folds or more over the chest and thrown back around the shoulders.

F

FAKIR: Holy men in drapes who rejected worldly goods for divinity.

G

GHUNGHAT: Veil or headscarf.

GHUNGHRUS: A type of bell found in India that is commonly used to decorate dresses or adorn anklets.

GOTTA: Type of metallic ribbon embroidery.

J

JAMA: Much longer than the Angrakha, this is a coat-like garment with a fitted bodice and a flaring lower half. It is usually full-sleeved and is tied under the armpits, often with lappets which could be a design feature in themselves.

JAMAWAR: Figured weave withal over paisley patterns in different coloured yarns to create rich tapestry patterns.

JADAU: Jewellery-making technique where precious gemstones are embedded into gold.

JIBBI: A plastic tongue cleaner.

JODHPURS: Close-fitting pants, especially around the calves, so they fit inside tall riding boots. Horse riders traditionally wear jodhpurs.

JUTTI: A traditional footwear.

K

KEDIYU: Frock-type kurta with frills, worn by men in rural Gujarat.

KALIDAR: Top made up of several geometrical pieces, similar to a frock but with many panels.

KANGRI JALI: A kind of mesh.

KANJIVARAM: Traditionally woven silk from Tamil Nadu.

KASAB: One of the oldest forms of embroidery, introduced from Persia. It looks similar to *zardozi* and is made with gold and silver fibres.

KHADI: Plain-weave fabric handwoven out of hand-spun cotton yarn. This fabric was promoted by Mahatma Gandhi during India's struggle for freedom.

KHAKHA: Tracing paper where small holes are punched on the outline of the motifs.

KHIRNI: A species of flowering tree native to the Indian subcontinent.

KIMKHAB: A type of brocade made in Benaras using gold and silk.

KUNDAN: A type of gold jewelry that typically has a wax core.

KURTA: Long loose-fitting collarless tunic, often extending to the knees.

KURTI: Short kurta.

L

LEHENGA: Full ankle-length pleated and embroidered skirt.

LUNGI: About 2½ yards of unstitched cotton that is folded about the body and tied at the waist.

M

MAHARANI: A great queen or wife of a maharaja.

MAL/MALMAL: A soft and fine cotton weave, also known as muslin.

MALKHA: A pure cotton cloth made directly from raw cotton in villages close to cotton fields.

N

NAGAS: Sadhus who worship Lord Shiva and mostly live in the Himalayas.

NAUVARI: Nine-yard sari that is tucked at the back.

P

PAITHANI: A variety or kind of sari that originated from Paithan – a small town in Maharashtra, these saris are hand-crafted with some of the finest silk.

PALLU: The loose end of a sari, worn over one shoulder or the head.

PARIKRAMA: Circumambulation of sacred entities.

PATOLA: A bright double ikat, usually silk from Gujarat that is made by dyeing the thread before weaving.

PESHAWARI: A traditional long frock worn by Memon women in Kutch.

PRÊT: Ready-to-wear fashion.

PICHWAI: A traditional art form that emerged in the 17th century at the Nathdwara Temple in Rajasthan.

PAJAMA: Trousers that are loose and have been worn in India since the Mughal rule are known as pyjamas.

Q

QAWWAL: A singer of qawwalis, a form of Sufi Islamic devotional songs originating in South Asia.

R

RESHAM: Silk.

S

SHAHTOOSH: High-quality wool from the neck hair of the Himalayan ibex.

SHERWANI: Coat-like garment that originated in Hyderabad in the late 19th century influenced by British cut and stitching. It is also influenced by the Indian achkan.

T

TABLA: A traditional percussion instrument, used widely in northern India.

TOILES PEINTES: Painted linen.

TOPI: Light hat or cap.

Z

ZARDOZI: Type of heavy and elaborate metal embroidery on a silk, satin, or velvet fabric base. Designs are often created using gold and silver threads.

Photo Credits

Published in India by Roli Books, 2023

M-75, Greater Kailash II Market, New Delhi-110 048, India.
E-mail: info@rolibooks.com, Website: www.rolibooks.com
Phone: ++91-11-40682000

ISBN: 9789392130878

DESIGN: PALLAVI NOPANY
EDITORS: PRIYA KAPOOR, NEELAM NARULA & NANDITA KRISHNAMURTHY
PRODUCTION: LAVINIA RAO

Printed and bound in India